D1529667

SOUP
GALORE

SOUP
GALORE

ELISABETH LUARD

spruce

An Hachette Livre UK Company

First published in Great Britain in 2009
by Spruce, a division of
Octopus Publishing Group Ltd
2–4 Heron Quays, London E14 4JP
www.octopusbooks.co.uk
www.octopusbooksusa.com

Distributed in the U.S. and Canada for
Octopus Books USA
c/- Hachette Book Group USA
237 Park Avenue
New York NY 10017.

Copyright © Octopus Publishing Group Ltd
    2009
Text copyright © Elisabeth Luard 2009

Elisabeth Luard asserts the moral right to be
identified as the author of this book.

ISBN 13 978-1-84601-329-4
ISBN 10 1-84601-329-1

A CIP catalog record of this book is available
from the Library of Congress.

Printed and bound in China

10 9 8 7 6 5 4 3 2

Photography: Ian Garlick
Food Styling: Felicity Barnham-Bobb,
    Eliza Baird
Page Layout: Balley Design Limited

All rights reserved. No part of this work
may be reproduced or utilized in any form
or by any means, electronic or mechanical,
including photocopying, recording, or by any
information storage and retrieval system,
without the prior written permission of
the publisher.

This book contains the opinions and ideas of
the author. It is intended to provide helpful
and informative material on the subjects
addressed in this book and is sold with the
understanding that the author and publisher
are not engaged in rendering any kind of
personal professional services in this book.
The author and publisher disclaim all
responsibility for any liability, loss, or risk,
personal or otherwise, which is incurred as
a consequence, directly or indirectly, of the
use and application of any of the contents
of this book.

CONTENTS

INTRODUCTION

Soup is the most undemanding of all culinary preparations. The only essentials are a large saucepan and enough water to submerge the ingredients—the rest is up to you—whether it is a simple soup designed to utilize the best of a single seasonal ingredient or a complex soup that depends on a dozen different ingredients and many layers of flavor you are making.

Anyone can make a soup, with or without a recipe. It's a dish for all seasons, enjoyed by everyone, eaten at any time day or night in company or alone. Soup is remarkably flexible in the making, and it is economical, too: whatever you choose to include gives its goodness to the broth and nothing is wasted.

It is also a comfort food. When there is a simmering pot of broth releasing its seductive perfume of herbs, onion, garlic, celery, peppercorns, fennel, ginger, lemon grass, orange zest—all's well with the world. Soul food or fuel food, call it what you will, soup is far more than a nourishing bowlful of goodness; soup speaks to the heart.

★ SOUPS AND TRADITION ★

Every culinary tradition on earth has its own idea of what a proper soup should be. In China and India soups feature regularly as part of the meal; soups are eaten in the tropical heat of Africa; there are seamen's soups, feasting soups for weddings, fasting soups for Ramadan, meatless soups for Lent, and chicken soup traditionally served in Jewish households as part of the Sabbath dinner.

There are soups for every situation: light soups to whet the appetite; delicate soups to tempt the unwell; strong soups for body-builders; hearty soups to fortify the field-worker; festive soups that are cooked only on special occasions; seductive soups perfect for those intimate occasions; leftover soups, revival soups, and survival soups.

But which is the best soup? It is the one that stays in the mind long after the taste has vanished—often the soup that just seemed to happen. The soup you made on the day the tomatoes achieved perfection; the chowder that virtually cooked itself when the fish was so fresh it jumped off the slab; the bone broth you made with a veal shin and a bacon knuckle and left to simmer all night by itself.

INGREDIENTS

There are soups for all the seasons: warming soups for winter, light soups for spring, chilled soups for summer, and soups that reflect the plenty of fall. Follow the calendar and choose what looks good in the market as your base ingredient, then have fun in the kitchen adding your preferred stock and seasonings to it.

★ SPRING ★

In spring, when the first young vegetables come into the stores but the weather is still chilly, stir green leaves —young spinach, shredded hearts of young cabbage or lettuce, lemony sorrel, and aniseed-flavored chervil—into a bean- or potato-based soup for freshness of flavor. Such soups go well with spring salads—new potatoes dressed with olive oil and chives; baby tomatoes tossed with basil and just a pinch of sugar; a well-minted tabbouleh with plenty of parsley and dressed with lemon juice. Take advantage, too, of the shellfish—oysters, clams, and mussels—that are plump and full of flavor at this time of year.

★ SUMMER ★

In summer, go for creamy soups that take well to chilling: vichyssoise, watercress or carrot soup, and pea soup finished with sour cream, for example. During really hot weather, serve a classic cold soup of the Mediterranean: red and white gazpacho or yogurt and cucumber soup,

KEEPING SOUPS

Clear soups and broths can be stored in the refrigerator for a week in a covered container—just give the broth a good boil-up before using. Thick soups should be well cooled before storing in the refrigerator and are better used within 2–3 days: vegetable matter, particularly onion, ferments in hot weather, although it all depends on your refrigerator and how often you open and close it.

well chilled and refreshingly diluted. For something different, experiment with fruit soups of north European tradition—blueberry, cherry, and apricot. Served cold, these soups are delicious with a spoonful of sour cream. Then there are fish soups a plenty, from the mighty bouillabaisse to a simple Greek *avgolemono* or the beautiful chowders of the Atlantic coastline—all a perfect choice for a summer dinner.

★ FALL ★

In fall, choose vegetable soups to deliver the sweet maturity of the harvest to the home—pumpkin, squash, corn, sweet potato, chestnuts, and wild mushrooms from the woods. As soon as the nights grow chilly, turn your thoughts to the delicately spiced, dhal-based soups of India. Also great at this time of year are the elegant noodle soups of China and Japan. Light but nourishing, they are particularly delicious when finished with shrimp, green chile, and coconut cream, as is done in Southeast Asia.

★ WINTER ★

As winter draws down, go for the robust bean or lentil soups, which remain the mainstay of the farmhouse kitchen, or choose one of the rich meat, poultry or bone-based broths that can, with the addition of root vegetables and pasta or dumplings, be served as a meal in themselves. When entertaining, start your menu with a well-flavored consommé, a sophisticated crab or lobster bisque, or one of the single-vegetable soups, such as tomato, beet, and French onion, which sharpen the palate without dulling the appetite.

PORTION SIZES

As a general rule of thumb, a one-person serving as a starter is considered to be 1¼ cups, although the volume should be halved if you are serving the soup followed by several courses.

★ COMBINING INGREDIENTS ★

While there is plenty of room for substitution within the classic soup recipes, it is useful to know what works well with what. For instance, that fava beans taste good with fennel, potato works well with leek, peas go perfectly with bacon, and corn with basil is a delicious combination. Nevertheless, however carefully you follow a recipe with such perfect combinations as these, experienced soup makers will tell you no soup ever turns out the same way twice.

★ ENHANCING THE FLAVOR ★

It is not only the ingredients used to make a soup that influence its flavor—the state of the weather, the temperament of the stove and the shape of the pot all have a part to play—and this is even before you choose the ingredients.

How you prepare the produce is also important when it comes to flavor. For example, should the onions be chopped or slivered or the carrots diced or chunked? Should the basic flavorings be fried before you add the liquid or should they be left to develop their fragrance in the simmering broth?

Your final decision when making a soup is in the tasting: the moment when an ordinary soup can rise to greatness. Too bland? Allow an extra five minutes bubbling to concentrate the flavors. Too thin? A quick mash with a fork will thicken the broth. Not lively enough? A stirring of chives, the addition of a little lemon zest, a lick of vinegar, a pinch of chile—any or all of these may do the trick.

EQUIPMENT

When making a soup it is not only the the cooking equipment you need to consider, you should also think about what you are going to serve the soup in.

★ COOKING EQUIPMENT ★

The basic equipment needed to make a soup includes a quart capacity saucepan, preferably with a heavy base to discourage burning, and a wooden spoon for stirring.

Essential too, is a small, sharp knife or potato-peeler for preparing the vegetables, a chopping knife, and a cutting board. You may also need a measuring cup—soup makers rarely use scales since proportions, unlike baking, don't need to be precise.

If you intend to make your own stock, you will need a large stockpot and strainer, and if the soup is to be reduced to a pureé, either a food processor or a potato-ricer will be required.

Although soups are essentially one-pot events occasionally there will be a need for a small frying pan.

★ SERVING EQUIPMENT ★

Presentation tells your guests what to expect. Hearty soups are best served directly from the pot in which they are cooked. Wide-rimmed soup plates are good if the soup has suckable debris—shells, bones, and the like—that will need to be discarded. Bowls, chosen for color and compatibility with the recipe, are good for pureés and other debris-free soups. Earthenware says the right thing about Mediterranean and Latin American recipes, while pottery is perfect for ordinary everyday vegetable, meat, and chicken soups. Bone china or porcelain is good for delicate Chinese, Japanese, and Southeast Asian soups, and for anything elegant and French.

No matter what dishes you use, they should be pre-warmed to help keep the heat of the soup.

SOUP STOCKS

Traditional soup recipes often call for a stockpot. In the days when big households ate together at least twice a day, the presence of a large pot bubbling gently on the back of the stove ensured the cook had the basis for a nourishing, healthy, economical meal that could be set on the table at short notice. These days with smaller households, irregular mealtimes, and changes in the way we buy our food, it is impractical to maintain this kind of old-fashioned stockpot. However, purpose-made stocks can be made in quantity and stored in the freezer.

FREEZING STOCK

To store a basic stock in the freezer, reduce it to half-volume (just simmer it down in an uncovered pan), pour it into ice-making trays, leave to cool, freeze till firm, then pop the cubes out of the trays and pack into bags till needed: they will last for at least three months (or follow your freezer directions), and can be diluted with their own volume of boiling water to bring them quickly back to life. Remember to label the bags—there is nothing more depressing than finding you have defrosted a fish stock when what you need is chicken.

★ BEEF STOCK ★

To prepare 1 quart meat stock you will need: *2¼ pounds sawn beef bones, 2¼ pounds beef shin, 2–3 carrots and celery ribs, 1 large onion, 1 bay leaf, 4–5 parsley sprigs, ½ teaspoon salt, ½ teaspoon peppercorns.*

Place the beef bones in a hot oven (400°F) until well browned. Transfer to a large stockpot with the beef shin. Chop the carrots and celery, and quarter the onion leaving the skin on. Add to the stockpot along with the bay leaf, parsley sprigs, salt, and pepper, and enough water to cover everything. Simmer for 2–3 hours, then strain out the solids and bubble up again until the liquid is reduced to about 1 quart. Strain the stock, discarding the solids, then leave to cool. Lift off the layer of creamy fat.

★ HAM OR BACON STOCK ★

To prepare 1½ quart ham or bacon stock you will need: *1 ham hock or bacon hock, 2–3 onions, 2–3 large carrots, 1 celeriac root, 4–5 parsley stalks, 1 bay leaf, ½ teaspoon peppercorns.*

Put the ham or bacon hock in a large stockpot. Roughly chop the onions, carrots, and celeriac, then add to the stockpot along with the parsley, bay leaf, and peppercorns. Pour in approximately 2 quarts of water and bring to a boil. Skim off the gray foam and add a spoonful of cold water to send the cloudy pieces to the bottom. Repeat this process twice more. Continue to simmer gently for about 1½ hours or until reduced by half. Strain the stock, discard the solids, and leave the stock to cool. Lift off the layer of creamy fat.

★ DASHI STOCK ★

To prepare 1 quart dashi stock you will need: *4in dried kombu (seaweed) and ¼ cup katsuo (dried bonito flakes)*

Put the kombu in a pan with 1 quart cold water and bring it very gently to a boil—remove the saucepan from the heat. Add 4 tablespoons cold water, then stir in the katsuo. Return the broth to the heat and bring back to a boil. Remove from the heat, cool, then strain.

★ CHICKEN STOCK ★

To prepare 1½ quarts chicken stock you will need:
4½ pounds chicken carcasses, necks, and wingtips,
2–3 carrots, 2–3 ribs celery sticks, 1 leek, 1 large onion,
5–6 parsley stalks, 1 bay leaf, ½ teaspoon salt, ½ teaspoon
peppercorns.

Break up the chicken carcasses and place in a hot oven (400°F) with the necks and wingtips until well browned. Remove from the oven and put them in a large stockpot. Chop the carrots, celery, and leek, and quarter the onion leaving the skin on. Add to the stockpot along with the parsley stalks, bay leaf, salt, and pepper, and enough water to submerge everything. Simmer very gently for 2–3 hours, skimming the fat from the surface every 20 minutes, then strain out the solids and bubble up again until the liquid is slightly reduced.

★ VEGETABLE STOCK ★

To prepare 1 quart vegetable stock you will need:
2 large onions, 1 fennel bulb, 3–4 ribs celery, 2 carrots,
2 bay leaves, ½ teaspoon salt, ½ teaspoon peppercorns,
2 quarts water.

Roughly dice the vegetables and place in a heavy stockpot with the bay leaves, salt, and pepper. Add the water, then bring the liquid to a boil. Simmer gently for about 1 hour or until the stock is reduced by half.

★ FISH STOCK ★

To prepare 1 quart fish stock you will need: *4½ pounds white fish bones and heads, 3–4 ribs celery, 1 fennel bulb, 2–3 leeks, 1 bay leaf, 1 thyme sprig, 2–3 parsley stalks, ¼ teaspoon white peppercorns, ½ teaspoon sea salt.*

Rinse the fish bones and heads and pack them into a large stockpot. Cover with 1½ quarts water and bring to a rolling boil. Skim off the gray foam that rises to the surface. Meanwhile, roughly chop the celery ribs, fennel bulb, and leeks. Add to the stockpot along with the remaining ingredients. Turn down the heat and simmer for 30 minutes—no longer or the stock will taste bitter. Strain the stock, discarding the solids.

FISH & SHELLFISH

NEW ENGLAND CLAM CHOWDER

SERVES 4–6

24 live clams
  (quahogs or steamers)
1/2 (4 tablespoons) stick butter
1/2 cup salt pork or
  unsmoked bacon, diced
2 onions, thinly sliced
1lb waxy white-fleshed
  potatoes, diced or sliced
2 cups milk
1lb cod fillet or other white
  fish fillet, skinned and diced
4–6 crackers (or matzos or
  water biscuits)
2/3 cup double cream
Salt and ground black pepper
Thick-cut brown bread, to serve

1. Rinse the clams, discarding any that don't retract the neck or feeder-tube when touched. Pop them in the freezer for 1–2 hours to make them easier to open. Lever the shells apart with a short, stout knife (do this over a bowl to catch the juice) and slip the fish off their shells. Remove the dark stomach, chop the meat and reserve.

2. Melt half the butter in a pan and fry the salt pork or bacon and onions gently until soft and golden—allow at least 10 minutes.

3. Add the potatoes and 1¼ cup water. Bring to a boil, turn down the heat and cover loosely. Simmer until the potatoes are nearly soft, about 10 minutes.

4. Add the milk and the reserved clam juice to the pan, return to a boil. Add the diced fish and poach for 2–3 minutes—just long enough for it to turn opaque. Break in the crackers.

5. Add the chopped shellfish meat with its juices. Heat everything together gently, stirring to marry the flavors. Remove from the heat and stir in the cream. Season to taste with salt and pepper.

6. Put a knob of butter into each soup dish before you pour in the hot chowder. Serve with thick-cut brown bread.

MR PICKWICK'S OYSTER SOUP

SERVES 4–6

12–18 oysters in the shell
2 cups fish stock (see page 16)
2 shallots or 1 small onion,
   finely chopped
$\frac{1}{2}$ cup white wine
1 bay leaf
2–3 parsley stalks
$\frac{1}{4}$ stick (2 tablespoons) unsalted
   butter
1 tablespoon all-purpose flour
1 cup heavy cream
1 teaspoon Worcestershire sauce
2–3 drops Tabasco sauce,
   plus extra to serve
Salt
Chopped onion, chives or parsley,
   to garnish

1. Hold each oyster over a fine sieve set over a bowl to catch the juices. With the oyster rounded shell up, insert the tip of an oyster knife, or a short, strong-bladed knife, into the hinge. Twist the knife to prise the hinge open and cut the muscles above and below the oyster. Cut between the shells to open them and cut away the oyster with a knife.

2. Bring the stock to a boil in a large saucepan and add the shallots or onion. Add the wine, bay leaf, and parsley stalks, and bubble up until the steam no longer smells of alcohol, about 10 minutes. Remove the bay leaf and parsley stalks.

3. Cream the butter with the flour and stir it into the hot broth. Whisk until smooth. Stir in the cream and the reserved oyster juices and bubble up again. Season with the Worcestershire sauce and Tabasco, taste and add salt.

4. Slip the oysters into the hot soup and return to just below boiling point. Ladle into bowls, dividing the oysters between each serving.

5. Garnish with a sprinkle of chopped raw onion, chives or parsley. Hand round more Tabasco sauce for anyone who likes their oysters peppery.

SHRIMP BISQUE

This velvety smooth soup, thickened with egg yolk and enriched with cream, is one of the glories of the French kitchen. Great as a light lunch served with a salad, hot baguette and unsalted French butter.

SERVES 4–6

1 cup raw shrimps
4 cups fish stock (see page 16)
¼ stick (2 tablespoons) unsalted butter
2 tablespoons all-purpose flour
1 teaspoon paprika
About 6 tablespoons heavy cream
3 egg yolks
Freshly grated nutmeg
Salt and ground black pepper

1. Shell the shrimps. Heat the stock in a saucepan with the shrimp debris and simmer for 15–20 minutes. Strain the broth and reserve.

2. Melt the butter in a large saucepan, stir in the flour and fry until it turns a sandy color—don't let it brown. Sprinkle in the paprika and remove from the heat. Gradually add the strained broth and whisk over a gentle heat until it thickens.

3. Remove the pan from the heat and whisk in the cream and egg yolks —you can do this in a food processor if you like.

4. Reheat gently, whisking all the while, until the soup is just below boiling point. Taste and season with nutmeg, salt and pepper.

5. Slip the shrimps into the soup and reheat until just below boiling point. Split between the bowls, making sure everyone gets their share of shrimps.

TIP
For a crab bisque, use cooked crab, white meat only, include a little mild paprika to spark up the color. Follow the same method.

LOBSTER OR CRAYFISH BISQUE

An elegant soup made with the debris of a crustacean feast is the perfect way to have your lobster and eat it, too. For a luxury version, serve each portion with a meaty claw on the side.

SERVES 4–6

6 lobster or crayfish shells,
   including all the debris
1 tablespoon sunflower oil
1 large leek, chunked
1 carrot, chunked
1 small fennel bulb, quartered
½ teaspoon black peppercorns
2–3 parsley sprigs
3 cups fish stock (see page 16)
⅔ white wine
½ stick (4 tablespoons) unsalted
   butter
1 tablespoon all-purpose flour
½ cup heavy cream
1 teaspoon tomato paste
½ teaspoon paprika
Salt and ground white pepper
Lobster or crayfish meat (optional),
   to serve

1. Preheat the oven to 450°F. Smash up the lobster or crayfish shells and spread all the debris in a roasting pan. Toss in the oil. Roast everything for 15–20 minutes, or until the shells and bits begin to brown—don't let anything burn.

2. Transfer the roasted debris to a large saucepan and add the leek, carrot, fennel (save the feathery greens), peppercorns, and parsley. Add the stock, wine, and 1 quart water. Bring to a boil, reduce the heat and leave to simmer very gently for 1 hour.

3. Strain the broth, pressing well to extract all the flavor, and return the stock to the pan. Bring it back to a boil and bubble up until you have 3 cups of well-flavored broth.

4. Meanwhile, cream the butter with the flour until well blended. Stir it into the hot broth and whisk over the heat for about 5–6 minutes, until the soup thickens a little and no longer tastes of raw flour.

5. Whisk in the cream, tomato paste, and paprika. Taste and add salt and freshly ground white pepper. Garnish with the reserved fennel green, finely chopped, and the lobster or crayfish meat, if using.

PORTUGUESE FISHERMAN'S SOUP

SERVES 6

6½lbs mixed soup fish, including rascasse (scorpion fish), conger eel, and dogfish (rock fish); also possible are skate, monkfish, red mullet, and sea bass

2¼lbs shellfish, such as cockles, mussels, clams, razor shells (optional)

⅔ cup olive oil

About 1½ cups white wine

1 tablespoon white wine vinegar

1 tablespoon mild pimentón (Spanish paprika)

1 tablespoon salt

2¼lbs potatoes, peeled and thickly sliced

2¼lbs ripe tomatoes, sliced

3–4 large onions, thinly sliced

3–4 garlic cloves, crushed with salt

1 bay leaf, crumbled

1. Prepare the fish as necessary (bone, scale, clean, and so on) and cut into thick steaks.

2. Rinse the shellfish, if using, then leave to soak for 3–4 hours until they spit out their sand. Scrape the beards from the mussels.

3. Have ready a large, deep-sided, flameproof casserole. In a bowl, mix the oil with the wine, vinegar, pimentón, and salt until well blended. If using shellfish, start with these, otherwise begin with the potatoes, layering the fish with the vegetables, garlic, and bay leaf to create as many layers as is convenient for the shape of the casserole. Pour over the oily dressing and leave to stand for 1–2 hours.

4. Carefully bring to a boil and cover as soon as steam begins to rise. Leave to simmer gently for an hour or so, or until all is tender—or transfer to the oven and bake at 325°F. Check occasionally and add boiling water, if necessary.

5. Let the stew cool a little before serving. When serving, push a spoon through all the layers so that each person gets a fragrant slice of everything.

SCOTTISH HADDOCK & POTATO SOUP

Otherwise known as Cullen Skink, this traditional Scottish soup was made by the fishermen of Cullen on the Moray Firth. Choose proper smoked haddock—pale, honey-colored, whole fish split down the bone and sold by the piece—rather than the bright yellow fillets.

SERVES 4–6

1 whole smoked haddock
   (about ¾lb)
2 leeks, thinly sliced
2¼lbs potatoes, sliced
3 cups whole milk
About ½ stick (4 tablespoons)
   unsalted butter, slivered
Chopped hard-boiled egg (optional)
Salt and ground black pepper
Chopped chives, to garnish

1. Put the haddock in a saucepan with enough water to cover. Bring to a boil, allow a big bubble, then remove the haddock with a slotted spoon. Skin and bone the fish, reserving the flesh, and discarding the rest. Flake the fish.

2. Put the leeks and potatoes in the pan with the cooking water. Add the milk and bring to a boil. Turn down the heat to a gentle simmer, season with salt and freshly ground pepper, and cook for 15–20 minutes, or until the potato is perfectly soft.

3. Stir in the reserved flaked fish and the butter, and reheat until just below boiling point. Stir in the chopped hard-boiled egg, if using. Taste and adjust the seasoning.

4. Ladle into soup bowls and garnish each portion with a sprinkle of chives.

SPANISH SHELLFISH SOUP WITH SHERRY

Quick and easy to make, this soup is a specialty of the seafront restaurants of Malaga. It's really only worth making when you have live shellfish in the shell—ready-cooked won't do for flavor and texture.

SERVES 4–6

2¼lbs live shellfish (bivalves
  —clams, mussels)
1 tablespoon olive oil
1–2 garlic cloves, slivered
2 tablespoons finely diced serrano
  ham or bacon
½ teaspoon saffron (about
  12 threads), toasted in a dry pan
1 tablespoon pimentón (Spanish
  paprika) or 1 Ñora (dried red
  pepper), seeded and torn
1 cup sherry (manzanilla or fino)
3 cups fish stock (see page 16)
Salt and ground black pepper
Chopped fresh Italian parsley,
  to garnish
TO SERVE
Quartered lemons
Fresh bread

1. Put the shellfish to soak in cold water to spit out their sand—overnight is best but 3–4 hours will do. Drain and rinse thoroughly. Scrape the beards from the mussels, if using.

2. Warm the olive oil in a large saucepan. Add the garlic and ham or bacon and fry for a moment until the garlic softens. Sprinkle with the saffron and the pimentón or Ñora. Stir over the heat for 1 minute, then add the sherry and bubble up for 2–3 minutes, or until the steam no longer smells of alcohol. Add the stock and bring to a boil.

3. Add the shellfish to the pan. Return to a boil, cover and cook for 3–4 minutes until the shellfish open. Discard any that remain closed. Remove the pan from the heat, taste, and adjust the seasoning.

4. Garnish with chopped parsley and serve without reheating, with quartered lemons and fresh bread for mopping. Provide a bowl for the debris.

SCOTTISH PARTAN BREE

SERVES 4–6

About 24 live swimmer crabs
   or 1 large cooked crab (with
   cooking water)
1 large pat of butter
1 medium onion, quartered
2 ribs celery, chopped
1 medium carrot, chunked
1 medium tomato, chopped
½ teaspoon crushed black
   peppercorns
4 tablespoons ginger wine or
   oloroso sherry
1 small bouquet garni (bay leaf,
   thyme, parsley, tied in a bunch)
Salt
2 egg yolks
4 tablespoons heavy cream
1 teaspoon paprika

1. If you are using swimmers, put the crabs in a bucket of fresh water and wait until they stop scuttling—they're seawater swimmers so fresh water sends them to sleep.

2. Melt the butter in a large saucepan. When it foams, gently fry the onion, celery, and carrot until soft. Add the tomato and increase the heat, stirring until it softens. Add 1 quart water, season with salt and the peppercorns, and bring to a boil.

3. If you are using swimmers, drain off the water and drop them straight into the boiling liquid—the heat will kill them instantly. If using cooked crab, remove the meat from the shell and add the debris to the pan, reserving the meat.

4. Add the wine or sherry and the bouquet garni. Bring the pan back to a boil and cover loosely. Reduce the heat and leave to simmer for about 40 minutes, or until the broth has reduced by one-third.

5. Remove the pan from the heat and leave to cool a little. If using swimmers, transfer everything to a food processor, process thoroughly, then pour back into the pan through a sieve. If using a large crab, strain to remove the crab debris before processing, then stir the reserved crab meat into the broth. Reheat gently until just below boiling point.

6. Meanwhile, whisk the egg yolks with the cream and paprika, then whisk in a ladleful of the nearly boiling broth. Stir the egg mixture back into the broth and stir over a low heat for a minute or two until it thickens a little. Check the seasoning and serve without reboiling.

BAHAMIAN CHOWDER

A robust, water-based chowder made with pumpkin and sweet potato and spiked with chile. Choose any combination of meaty fish. Delicious, too, when made with the clawless Caribbean lobster—use the shells for the stock and the meat to finish the soup.

SERVES 4

1¼lbs fresh swordfish steaks, diced
1¼lbs fresh tuna steaks, diced
3 cups fish stock (see page 16)
1lbs tomatoes, peeled, seeded,
    and diced
⅛ stick (1 tablespoon) butter
6–8 allspice berries, roughly crushed
1–2 Scotch bonnet chiles, seeded and
    chopped (or ½ teaspoon dried
    chiles, torn)
1lb sweet potato, diced
1lb pumpkin, diced
Salt and ground black pepper
TO SERVE
Quartered limes or lemons
Tabasco

1. Salt the fish lightly and set it aside.

2. Put the fish stock in a large saucepan and bring it to a boil.

3. Meanwhile, fry the tomatoes in the butter until the flesh collapses. Add the allspice and chiles and fry for another minute.

4. Tip the contents of the pan into the boiling fish stock. Add the sweet potato and pumpkin and return to a boil. Cover loosely and bubble up for 15–20 minutes, or until the vegetables are tender.

5. Slip in the fish, reheat, and simmer for 3–4 minutes, or until the flesh turns opaque—don't overcook it.

6. Taste and adjust the seasoning. Ladle into bowls and serve with quartered limes or lemons for squeezing, and Tabasco on the side.

BRETON CHOWDER

The *cotriade*, Brittany's very own fish chowder, is served in two parts: the broth is drunk first and the fish and potatoes are served afterward.

SERVES 4–6

FOR THE FISH
The fish (gutted and scaled but
   left whole):
2 medium mackerel
3 smallish gurnard
1lb conger eel
2 whiting or codling
1 small sea bream

FOR THE BROTH
1 tablespoon unsalted butter or
   pork lard
2 medium onions, chopped
2–3 garlic cloves, chopped
2¼lbs potatoes, chopped into
   bite-sized pieces
1 cup soft-leaved herbs (chervil,
   sorrel, parsley, chives), shredded
Salt and ground black pepper

TO SERVE
Baguette or any crusty French bread
Unsalted French butter, melted, or
   a vinaigrette made with Dijon
   mustard, olive oil and wine vinegar

1. Rinse the fish and break it into bite-sized pieces, discarding the heads if you feel you must. Salt lightly and set aside in a cool place.

2. For the broth, melt the butter or lard in a large saucepan. Add the onions and garlic and fry gently until softened and golden. Add 1 quart water, bring to a boil and add the potatoes and a little salt. Return to a boil, reduce the heat and cover the pan. Simmer for 20 minutes, or until the potatoes are tender.

3. Stir in the shredded herbs and check the seasoning. Return to a boil and lay the fish pieces in the broth. Cover and cook for 3–4 minutes, or until the fish flesh has firmed and turned opaque—don't overcook it.

4. Serve the broth first, ladled into deep soup plates in which you have placed a slice or two of bread. Serve the fish and potatoes in the same plate with melted butter or a vinaigrette to moisten.

TIP
Breton fishermen will tell you a cotriade is unthinkable without a bottle of full-bodied red wine to enable you to faire chabrot— dilute the last drops of soup in the bowl with wine, swirl it about, and drink the tasty mix down.

NORMANDY FISH SOUP

SERVES 4–6

About 1 pound whole flatfish (such
    as plaice, sole, small turbot),
    cleaned
About 1 pound bony white fish (such
    as conger eel, gurnard, whiting),
    cleaned
½ stick (4 tablespoons) unsalted
    butter
½ cup mushrooms (chanterelles,
    if you can get them), roughly
    chopped, or ⅓ cup dried
    chanterelles, soaked for
    20 minutes in warm water
2 tablespoons Calvados or apple
    brandy
1 cup dry cider
2 cups fish stock (see page 16)
1¼lbs live mussels, soaked, scrubbed,
    and bearded
1 tablespoon flour creamed with
    1 tablespoon butter
½ cup heavy cream
2–3 tarragon sprigs or a handful of
    chervil, chopped

1. Prepare the fish as you please. Fillet or chop it, or leave it whole,
depending on the size of the fish and your guests' preferences.

2. Melt the butter in a large saucepan and add the mushrooms and fish.
Fry gently, turning the fish once, until lightly browned.

3. Pour the Calvados or brandy over the contents of the pan and light the
alcohol with a match. Wait until the alcohol burns off, then add the cider
and the stock.

4. Bring rapidly to a boil and gently place the mussels on top of the fish.
Cover and wait for 5 minutes for the shells to open in the steam.

5. Transfer the fish and mussels to deep soup plates. Discard any mussels
that remain closed.

6. Reheat the broth. Stir in the creamed flour and butter and bubble up
for 3–4 minutes, whisking until the broth thickens a little. Stir in the
cream and bubble up again. Stir in the herbs and ladle the creamy broth
over the fish.

CAMBODIAN HOT & SOUR FISH SOUP

Quickly prepared, fiery with chile, and soured with lemon, this is a soup that depends on the quality of the stock, which should be freshly made with the bones and heads of white-fleshed fish only.

SERVES 4—6

2 garlic cloves, crushed

1 slice of fresh ginger root, finely chopped

1 lemon grass stalk, chopped

1 quart fish stock (see page 16)

½ teaspoon salt

8ozs white fish steaks

4ozs rice vermicelli or other soup noodles

1–2 green chiles, seeded and thinly sliced

Juice of 1 lime

1. In a saucepan, simmer the garlic, ginger, and lemon grass in the fish stock for 20 minutes. Meanwhile, salt the fish lightly on both sides, cover with plastic wrap and leave in a cool place while the stock cooks.

2. Strain the stock and return it to the pan. Bring back to a boil and add the fish steaks.

3. Return the soup to a boil and drop in the vermicelli or soup noodles. Bubble gently for 2–3 minutes, until the noodles are soft and the fish has turned opaque. Season with the chiles and the lime juice and serve.

BERGEN FISH SOUP

SERVES 6

4 cod steaks (weighing about
    4ozs each) or 8ozs raw jumbo
    prawns
1 medium-sized cod roe
    (about 12ozs)
1 quart fish stock (see page 16)
1½lbs potatoes, peeled and diced
1 medium onion, thinly sliced
1 thick slice of ham, diced finely
¼ stick (2 tablespoons) butter
1lb live mussels, soaked, scrubbed,
    and bearded
2 egg yolks
2 tablespoons heavy cream
Salt and ground black pepper
TO GARNISH
A few dill sprigs
1 tablespoon pickled onions, diced

1. Wipe over the cod steaks and salt them lightly. Rinse the cod roe and wrap in a double envelope of waxed paper. Bring a pan of salted water to a boil and slip in the packet of roe. Bring back to a boil, then turn down the heat. Simmer until the roe is firm—a medium-sized roe takes about 25 minutes. Leave it in the water to cool. Unwrap and slice thickly.

2. In a large saucepan, bring the fish stock to a boil with the potatoes. Turn down the heat and cover loosely. Simmer for 10–15 minutes, or until the potatoes are nearly tender. Meanwhile, fry the onion and ham gently in the butter in a small frying pan until the onion is soft and golden.

3. Tip the contents of the frying pan into the soup and lay the mussels on top. Bring back to a boil, cover, and cook for 5 minutes (just enough to open the mussels).

4. Carefully, with a slotted spoon, transfer the solids to a warmed, deep soup tureen. Discard any mussels that remain closed. Slip the cod steaks into the broth and let them poach for 3–4 minutes, or until firm, then transfer to the tureen.

5. Whisk the egg yolks with the cream. Whisk in a ladleful of the boiling broth. Stir this back into the soup and reheat gently—don't let it boil or the egg will scramble. Taste and add salt and pepper. Pour the soup over the fish and vegetables and cod roe, and sprinkle with chopped dill and a few diced pickled onions.

SARDINIAN FISH SOUP WITH SAFFRON

A simple shrimp and mussel soup flavored with saffron, a flavoring much favored by Mediterranean cooks. Serve with plenty of rough bread for mopping.

SERVES 4–6

1 knifetip of saffron (about 20 threads)
4 cups fish stock (see page 16)
1 large onion, diced
1 carrot, diced
1–2 bay leaves
1/2 teaspoon crushed peppercorns
1lb live mussels or clams, soaked, scrubbed, and if using mussels, bearded
8ozs white fish fillets (swordfish, bass, mullet, hake)
8ozs large raw prawns or shrimp
Salt

TO GARNISH
1 teaspoon grated lemon zest
1 tablespoon chopped fresh parsley

1. Toast the saffron in a dry pan until the scent rises, about 2–3 minutes.

2. In a large saucepan, bring the fish stock to a boil with the onion, carrot, bay leaves, and peppercorns. Crush the saffron into a spoonful of boiling water—use the back of a spoon—and stir it into the stock.

3. Reheat the stock to just boiling and add the mussels or clams. Return the broth to a boil and cover to let the shells open in the steam, discarding any that do not open.

4. Remove the lid, add the fish fillets, and poach them for 2–3 minutes, or until the flesh is firm and opaque.

5. Add the shrimp to the pan. Return the mixture to a boil and remove from the heat. Taste and adjust the seasoning.

6. Ladle into warm soup plates and garnish with a sprinkle of lemon zest and chopped parsley.

HUNGARIAN FISH SOUP WITH PAPRIKA

SERVES 4–6

About 6½lbs river fish (carp, perch, tench) or any white-fleshed sea fish (cod, haddock)

2¼lbs onions, finely chopped

1 teaspoon dill or fennel seeds

2 heaped tablespoons mild paprika

2ozs egg noodles

Salt

1 tablespoon chopped fresh dill, to garnish

TO SERVE

1 level tablespoon chile powder

⅔ cup sour cream

Country bread

1. Rinse the small fish and gut but don't scale them. Behead and gut the larger fish and cut them into thick cutlets.

2. Put the small fish and the heads of the larger ones into a large saucepan. Add 4½ cups litres water and bring to a boil. Reduce the heat and simmer uncovered for 1 hour, or until the fish is mushy.

3. Push the broth through a sieve or potato ricer, making sure all the little threads of flesh drop through, but leaving the bones behind.

4. Return the broth to the pan and add the onions, dill or fennel seeds, and the paprika. Stir, bring to the boil, reduce the heat, and cover loosely. Simmer gently for 30 minutes, or until the onions are perfectly tender. Taste and bring up the flavor with salt (freshwater fish has no natural salt). Add the noodles and bubble up and cook until soft.

5. Add the larger fish cutlets and poach them gently in the fish broth until firm and opaque—they will need only 3–4 minutes.

6. Divide the broth and fish among 4–6 warmed bowls and garnish with chopped dill. Mix a ladleful of the hot broth with the chile powder and hand it round separately. Serve with sour cream and plenty of country bread for mopping.

BOUILLABAISSE

Marseilles is the home of this famous fish soup, which takes its name from the method of cooking rather than, as is more usual with such venerable dishes, the cooking pot. A *bouillon-abaissé* is a broth whose heat is raised and lowered, then raised again—a process that encourages the broth to form an emulsion with the oil. The fish is variable, though it's generally agreed that rascasse, a rock fish with particularly gluey bones, should be included.

SERVES 4–6

FOR THE FISH

The fish (you need 6½lbs of at least 5 different varieties, one of which must be a rock fish). Choose from:

Rascasse

Sea bass

Monkfish

Scorpion fish

John Dory

Conger eel

Red mullet or goatfish

Red gurnard

Whiting

Weever fish

Crawfish

Shrimps

Crayfish

Steak fish such as tuna, turbot, large mackerel, bonito

1. Scale, trim, and bone the fish as appropriate (or have your fishmonger do this for you), reserving the heads and bones. Cut the larger fish into pieces roughly the same size as the smaller fish.

2. Divide the fish between two plates. The first plate should have firm-fleshed fish such as rascasse, weever, gurnard, eel, monkfish, swordfish, and the crustaceans. The second plate should have the soft-fleshed fish, such as sea bass and whiting.

3. For the broth, put the fish debris, shallots or leeks, garlic, chopped tomatoes, herbs, orange zest, and saffron in a large soup pot with about 3 quarts water. Bring to a boil and add salt and a few peppercorns. Reduce the heat and simmer for 20–30 minutes to extract all the flavor and body. Strain the broth and return it to the pot with the potatoes. Bring all back to a boil.

4. Warm a soup tureen and a large serving dish along with sufficient soup plates for all, and tell everybody you'll be ready in exactly 25 minutes.

FOR THE BASIC BROTH

Bones, heads, trimmings from the
   above, including whole fish if small

3–4 shallots or leeks, chopped

3–4 garlic cloves, crushed

2 large tomatoes, peeled, seeded,
   and chopped

3–4 sprigs each of fennel, parsley
   and thyme

1 strip of dried orange zest

About 12 saffron threads

6 white peppercorns, crushed

3–4 large, oval, yellow-fleshed
   potatoes, quartered

About $\frac{2}{3}$ cup extra virgin olive oil

Salt and ground black pepper

TO SERVE

1 quantity rouille (see Tip)

3–4 day-old bread rolls, halved
   lengthways

1 garlic clove

Fresh bread

5. As soon as the broth and potatoes have come back to the boil, allow 15 minutes for the potatoes to soften. Add the firm-fleshed fish from the first plate, starting with the crustaceans. Sprinkle with the olive oil, cover the pot again and bring swiftly back to a boil. Boil rapidly for 5 minutes. Lay in the soft fish from the second plate. Bring swiftly back to a boil and continue boiling briskly, uncovered, for another 5 minutes.

6. Take the pot off the heat, remove the fish with a slotted spoon and transfer it to the serving dish.

7. Have the rouille ready in a warm bowl. Toast the bread, rub with a cut clove of garlic, spread with a little rouille, and place the slices in the warm tureen. Dilute the remainder of the rouille with a ladleful of hot broth. Ladle a little of the broth over the bread in the tureen and wait until it goes spongy, 1–2 minutes. Ladle in the rest of the broth.

8. Set the tureen, fish platter, and rouille bowl on the table. Provide a warm soup plate and a fork and spoon for each guest, along with a large napkin, finger bowls, and a communal plate for the little bones. Hand out more bread, untoasted, to accompany. Everyone eats as he or she pleases, helping themselves from the tureen, fish platter and the rouille.

ROUILLE

Toast 2 red bell peppers, whole, in a very hot oven for 15 minutes. Remove from the oven and put them into a plastic bag for 20 minutes. Scrape the flesh from the skin. Crush 4 garlic cloves with $\frac{1}{2}$ teaspoon salt. Soak 1 thick slice of dry bread in a little water, then squeeze dry. Blend all ingredients together in a food processor.

SINGAPOREAN SHRIMP & COCONUT SOUP WITH RICE NOODLES

SERVES 4–6

8ozs rice vermicelli

4 tablespoons oil (sesame or soy)

4ozs beansprouts, trimmed of any brown bits

1 teaspoon finely chopped lemon grass

2 tablespoons dried shrimp paste or fish sauce, or 2 salted anchovies

2 small onions or shallots, finely chopped

1 teaspoon ground turmeric

2$\frac{1}{2}$ cups coconut milk

8ozs shrimp, shelled

Salt

4–6 small mint sprigs, to garnish

TO SERVE

1 lime, quartered

Fresh green or red chile, seeded and sliced

1. Soak the rice vermicelli in a bowl of very hot water for 10 minutes to swell, then drain and toss with 1 tablespoon of the oil. Divide the noodles among 4 soup bowls, top with the beansprouts and set aside.

2. Drop the remainder of the oil into a food processor. Add the lemon grass and shrimp paste (or fish sauce or anchovies, if using) with the onions or shallots and turmeric and process to a paste.

3. Fry the mixture gently in a large saucepan until the mixture smells fragrant, stirring to prevent burning. Add the coconut milk, bubble up, and add the shrimp. Bubble up again for just long enough for the shrimp to turn opaque. Taste and add salt.

4. Ladle the soup over the vermicelli and the beansprouts and garnish each portion with a mint sprig. Serve with the quartered lime for squeezing and chopped chile for those who like it hot.

CATALAN FISH SOUP

SERVES 4 AS A MAIN DISH

1lb live mussels, soaked, scrubbed,
   and bearded
1lb monkfish tail, filleted
1lb sea bream, filleted
12ozs squid, cleaned
2–3 tablespoons plain flour
100ml olive oil
1 small onion, thinly sliced
2 garlic cloves, finely slivered
1lb ripe tomatoes, peeled,
   seeded, and diced
1 short cinnamon stick
About 12 saffron threads, toasted
   in a dry pan
1 small glass dry sherry or
   white wine
12 large raw shrimp or langoustines
Salt and ground black pepper
2 tablespoons chopped fresh parsley,
   to garnish

1. Scrape the mussels and remove their beards. Put them in a large saucepan with 2 cups lightly salted water.

2. Bring to a boil, cover and cook for 5 minutes or until the shells open. Remove the pan from the heat and transfer the mussels with a slotted spoon to a warm serving dish. Discard any mussels that remain closed.

3. Strain the broth through a cloth-lined sieve—mussels are hard to rid of all their sand. Set aside.

4. Chop the fish fillets into bite-sized pieces and slice the squid into rings, leaving the tentacles in a bunch. Dust the fish through a plateful of seasoned flour.

5. Heat the oil in a large frying pan. Fry the floured fish for 2–3 minutes on each side, until firm and golden. Transfer to the serving dish with the mussels. Reheat the pan and gently fry the onion and garlic until it softens—don't let it brown.

6. Add the tomatoes, cinnamon, and saffron and bubble up until the tomato collapses, mashing it down to make a thick sauce. Add the sherry or wine and bubble up to evaporate the alcohol.

7. Add the mussel broth and bubble up stirring to blend. Taste and season with pepper.

8. Lay the shrimp in the hot broth, bubble up and cook briefly until they turn opaque, then transfer the shrimp to the serving dish.

9. Bubble up the sauce again until thick and rich. Ladle the sauce over the fish and garnish with a generous sprinkling of parsley.

GREEK FISH SOUP WITH EGG AND LEMON

SERVES 4–6

About 4½lbs white fish, scaled and
    gutted but left whole
4 tablespoons olive oil
2–3 ribs celery (green, unblanched),
    chopped
1 large onion, thinly sliced
2 tomatoes, peeled and chopped
1lb large new potatoes, quartered
    lengthways
2 egg yolks
Juice of 1 large lemon
Salt and ground black pepper
1–2 lemons, quartered, to serve

1. Salt the fish thoroughly and set it aside. Bring 4 cups water to a boil in a large saucepan with the oil, celery, onion, tomatoes, and new potatoes. Cover loosely and simmer for about 15 minutes, or until the potatoes are nearly soft.

2. Rinse the salt off the fish and lay it carefully on top of the potatoes. Bring the broth back to a boil, reduce the heat, and cover the pan. Cook for another 8–12 minutes, or until the potatoes are perfectly tender and the fish is done—you will have to judge this for yourself by parting the flesh down the backbone with a knife: the bone should no longer be pink.

3. Carefully lift out the fish and vegetables with a slotted spoon. Season to taste and divide among 4–6 warm soup bowls.

4. Whisk the egg yolks with the lemon juice in a bowl. Whisk in a ladleful of the hot broth. Remove the pan from the heat and whisk in the frothy egg mixture. Ladle the broth over the fish in the bowls. Serve with the lemon quarters.

BRAZILIAN MUSSEL SOUP

This elegant mussel soup from Bahia, Brazil's manufacturing hub, is based on a wine-flavored broth enriched with coconut milk, flavored with orange zest, and fortified with rice.

SERVES 4–6

2½lbs live mussels, soaked, scrubbed, and bearded
1 cup dry white wine
1 bay leaf
3 tablespoons extra virgin olive oil
1 large onion, chopped
2 garlic cloves, finely chopped
4ozs long-grain white rice
1lb tomatoes, peeled and chopped, or canned plum tomatoes
1 strip of orange zest (finger-length)
1 tablespoon chopped fresh parsley
1 tablespoon chopped fresh basil
1 teaspoon chopped fresh cilantro
1¼ cups unsweetened coconut milk
Salt and ground black pepper

TO SERVE
2 tablespoons olive oil
1 teaspoon paprika
Piri-piri or chili sauce

1. Scrub the mussels and scrape off the beards when you are ready to cook them. Bring the wine to a boil with the bay leaf in a large saucepan. Add the mussels, return the pan to a boil, and cover. Cook over a high heat for long enough to open the mussels, 5–6 minutes.

2. Remove the mussels, discarding any that remain closed. Strain and reserve the liquor.

3. Heat the oil in a heavy pan over a medium heat and sauté the onion and garlic until translucent. Add the rice and turn it in the hot oil. Add the tomatoes and let it all bubble up for a couple of minutes.

4. Add the orange zest, mussel liquor, and 1 quart boiling water to the pan. Bring to a boil and cover. Simmer for 10 minutes, stirring from time to time.

5. Stir in the parsley, basil, and cilantro, and season with salt and pepper. Simmer for another 5 minutes, then stir in the coconut milk. Bring back to a boil, add the mussels, and continue cooking until the rice is tender— a few minutes more.

6. Serve the soup in deep plates and finish with a trickle of olive oil blended with a little paprika (*dende*—palm oil—is traditional). Hand round piri-piri or chili sauce separately.

SCOTTISH TWEED KETTLE

A classic fish soup made with salmon, the Tweed Kettle takes its name from Scotland's most famous sporting river. Take care not to overcook the fish—it needs just long enough for the flesh to turn opaque.

SERVES 4

4–6 salmon steaks (about 4ozs each)
1½lbs potatoes, sliced
1 large onion, thinly sliced
2 tablespoons chopped chives
Salt and ground black pepper

FOR THE BUTTER SAUCE

¾ cup butter
1 tablespoon vinegar
2 hard-boiled eggs, freshly chopped

1. Wipe over the salmon steaks, salt them lightly, and set them aside.

2. Place half the potatoes in the bottom of a heavy saucepan, cover with the sliced onion and top with the remaining potatoes. Pour in enough boiling water to cover the potatoes completely—about 2 quarts—and add 1 teaspoon salt.

3. Bring the pan to a boil, cover tightly, and simmer for 30 minutes. Alternatively, you can use a casserole and cook the potato mixture in the oven preheated to 350°F. You may need to add a little more boiling water. Five minutes before the end of the cooking time, lay the salmon steaks on top of the potatoes and season with generous amounts of pepper.

4. Return the broth to a boil and cover. The fish will take no longer than 5 minutes to cook through. Stir in the chopped chives.

5. To make the butter sauce, melt the butter in a small pan, whisk in the vinegar and stir in the chopped hard-boiled eggs.

6. Ladle the potatoes, onion, and salmon steaks into warm serving bowls and hand round the butter sauce separately.

POULTRY
& GAME

CHICKEN CONSOMMÉ

One of the simplest and most elegant of starters is a chicken consommé flavored as they like to make it in France—with celery and tarragon. Perfect if you are feeling unwell and for babies.

SERVES 6–8

2¼lbs chicken joints (drumsticks or wings)
2 onions, chopped
4–5 ribs celery, chopped
2 quarts strained chicken stock (see page 16)
1 strip of lemon zest
1–2 tarragon sprigs
3 egg whites, well whisked
Salt

TIP
To make 1 quart good, strong chicken stock, allow 2¼lbs chicken wing tips and necks to 1½ litres water; flavor with leek-tops, carrot, bay, peppercorns, and allspice; cover loosely and simmer without letting bubbles break the surface for 3–4 hours until reduced by one-third.

1. Rinse the chicken joints and pack them into a large saucepan with the onions, celery, and stock. Bring to a boil and leave to simmer gently for 2 hours, or until the chicken has given up all its goodness and the broth has reduced by half.

2. Add the lemon zest and tarragon and leave to infuse on the side of the stove for 10 minutes. Strain the broth, discarding the solids.

3. Return the broth to the pan, bring it back to a boil, and whisk in the egg whites. Bring the liquid back to a boil, reduce the heat, and simmer for 20 minutes, or until the egg white floats to the top, collecting the impurities on the way.

4. Remove the pan from the heat and strain the broth through a sieve lined with a clean cloth. Blot the surface with paper towels to remove any lingering bubbles of fat.

5. To serve, reheat until just boiling, taste, and add salt.

SPANISH FIFTEEN-MINUTE SOUP

A simple, nourishing soup that is quickly prepared using a strong chicken or meat stock, or even a ladleful of broth from the midday bean-pot. It is popular all over Spain with recipes varying from region to region. In Andalusia, mint is sometimes added to the broth to give a Moorish flavor.

SERVES 4–6

1 quart chicken, beef, or ham stock
   (see pages 15 and 16)
2 tablespoons diced serrano ham
3ozs vermicelli or angel-hair pasta
2 hard-boiled eggs, diced
1 tablespoon fresh chopped parsley
1 tablespoon fresh chopped mint

1. Bring the chicken, beef, or ham stock to a boil in a saucepan with the diced serrano ham. Reduce the heat and simmer for 10 minutes.

2. Add the vermicelli or angel-hair pasta. Stir and return to a boil. Simmer for 3–4 minutes, or until the pasta is soft.

3. Remove from the heat and stir in the diced eggs, parsley, and mint. Ladle into soup bowls.

CHICKEN SOUP WITH SAFFRON & RICE

SERVES 4–6

1lb chicken joints
2 large carrots, scraped and diced
1lb turnips, peeled, and diced
2 large leeks, finely sliced
3–4 ribs celery, chopped
1 small onion, quartered
2–3 cloves
$\frac{1}{2}$ teaspoon white peppercorns
Bouquet garni: 1 small bunch of bay
    leaf, rosemary, marjoram, thyme
About $\frac{3}{4}$ cup round-grain rice
$\frac{1}{2}$ teaspoon saffron soaked in
    1 tablespoon boiling water
2 ripe tomatoes, skinned, seeded,
    and diced
Salt and ground black pepper

1. Put the chicken in a large saucepan with the vegetables, spices, and herbs. Season with salt.

2. Add water to cover—you will need at least 2 quarts. Bring the water to a boil, cover the pan, and turn down to a simmer. Leave to cook gently (no large bubbles should break the surface) for 30–40 minutes, until the chicken meat is dropping off the bones and the broth is well flavored.

3. Strain the broth through a sieve placed over a bowl. Discard the vegetables, and pick the chicken meat off the bones and reserve.

4. Return the broth to the pan and bring it back to a boil. Stir in the rice. Add the saffron and its soaking water (for added potency, drop the saffron and its water in the blender and process briefly).

5. Return to a boil, lower the heat, and simmer for 20–30 minutes, until the rice is perfectly tender and the broth has turned a sunny gold.

6. Taste and season, then stir in the diced tomato and the reserved chicken meat.

7. Reheat the soup and ladle it into bowls—white, for preference, the better to admire the color—making sure everyone gets their share of rice and chicken.

CHINESE EGG-FLOWER SOUP

This delicate soup is designed to please the eye as well as the palate. The egg is swirled into the hot broth without any more cooking, letting it set in soft petal shapes.

SERVES 4–6

1 quart clear chicken stock
(see page 16)
1 slice of fresh ginger root, pressed
to extract the juice
2 tablespoons Chinese rice wine or
dry sherry
1 teaspoon sesame oil
2 large eggs, forked to blend
2–3 spring onions, trimmed and
sliced diagonally, to garnish

1. In a medium saucepan, bring the stock gently to a boil with the ginger juice, rice wine or sherry, and sesame oil.

2. Using a pair of chopsticks or a slotted spoon, swirl the stock in a clockwise direction and pour in the beaten egg. Immediately remove from the heat and swirl the soup in the opposite direction so that the egg makes a flowery pattern.

3. Ladle into soup bowls and garnish each portion with a sprinkling of sliced spring onion.

VIETNAMESE CHICKEN BROTH WITH LEMON GRASS & GINGER

A plain chicken broth is infused with lemon grass and given a little heat with fresh ginger; warming in winter and an excellent cure for colds.

SERVES 4–6

1 quart chicken stock (see page 16)
1 lemon grass stalk, trimmed and
  chopped
1 slice of fresh ginger root, shredded
1oz cellophane noodles
Quartered limes, to serve
TO GARNISH
2–3 cilantro sprigs, leaves only
1 green chile, seeded, and thinly
  sliced

1. Put the chicken stock, lemon grass, and ginger in a large saucepan and bring to a boil. Remove from the heat and leave to infuse for 20 minutes.

2. Meanwhile, soak the noodles in warm water for 15 minutes to swell.

3. Strain the flavored broth, discarding the lemon grass and ginger. Return the broth to the pan and reheat until boiling. Add the noodles, bring back to a boil and simmer for 5 minutes.

4. Ladle the soup and noodles into small soup bowls and garnish each portion with a few cilantro leaves and sliced green chile. Serve with quartered limes for squeezing.

COLOMBIAN HEARTY CHICKEN SOUP

Colombia's national dish, the *sancocho*, is made with a whole chicken, ideally an elderly boiling fowl, poached in much the same way as France's *poule au pot*, but finished with Latin American ingredients, cassava and plantain, and served with a green salsa.

SERVES 4–6

1½ quarts chicken stock
   (see page 16)
1lb cassava, peeled and diced
1lb yellow-fleshed potatoes, peeled
   and diced
½lb chicken breast fillet, diced
1 plantain or unripe banana, skinned,
   and diced
2 tablespoons corn kernels
Salt

FOR THE SALSA
2ozs fresh cilantro
6 spring onions, diced
1 teaspoon ground cumin
4 tablespoons lemon or lime juice
2 fresh chiles, seeded and diced

TO SERVE
Quartered lemons or limes
Fresh tortillas

1. Bring the stock to a boil in a large saucepan with the cassava and potatoes. Skim off any foam that rises, reduce the heat, and cover loosely. Simmer for 20–30 minutes, or until the potatoes and cassava are tender.

2. Add the diced chicken and plantain or banana. Return to a boil, reduce the heat, and cook for another 10 minutes, or until the chicken is firm. Stir in the corn, reheat until boiling, then remove the pan from the heat. Taste and add salt.

3. To make the salsa, transfer a ladleful of the hot broth to a food processor and add all the salsa ingredients. Process until you have a fragrant, peppery green sauce. Either stir this into the soup or hand it round separately. Serve with lemon or lime quarters and warm tortillas.

GOOSE & NAVY BEAN SOUP

SERVES 4–6

1 piece of goose or duck confit
  (leg or wing)
1lb cooked navy or cannellini beans
  (canned is fine)
1 quart beef or chicken stock
  (see pages 15 and 16)
2 garlic cloves, chopped
2 tablespoons tomato paste
Salt and ground black pepper

FOR THE CROÛTONS

1 teaspoon dried thyme
1 teaspoon dried marjoram
4–5 tablespoons stale bread, cubed
Butter or oil, if necessary

1. In a frying pan, gently heat the goose or duck confit until the fat runs. Save the fat. Separate the meat with its skin from the bones. Shred the meat and skin and reserve.

2. Put the bones in a saucepan with the cooked beans. Add the stock, garlic, and the tomato paste and bring to the boil. Skim off any gray foam that rises, turn the heat down to a simmer and cook gently for about 30 minutes, or until the beans are mushy.

3. Put half the beans and a ladleful of the cooking broth in a food processor and process to a purée, adding more broth if the beans clog up the blades. Stir the purée back into the soup. Taste and adjust the seasoning. Dilute with a little boiling water if necessary—the soup should be thick enough to hold the croûtons.

4. Meanwhile, melt the reserved goosefat in a small frying pan and fry the shredded goose meat briefly until the skin crisps and the meat browns. Remove and reserve. Add the herbs and bread cubes to the pan (you may need a little butter or oil) and stir them over the heat until they absorb the fat and the fragrance of the herbs. Continue to stir until they are crisp.

5. Reheat the bean soup and ladle into warm bowls. Serve with crisp goose meat and herby croûtons.

NORMANDY PHEASANT SOUP WITH CHESTNUTS & CREAM

SERVES 4

1 mature pheasant, cleaned and
  jointed
½ stick (4 tablespoons) unsalted
  butter
1 large onion, diced
⅔ cup dry champagne or white wine
Bay leaf
1 thyme sprig
½ teaspoon ground allspice
1lb peeled chestnuts
2 cups heavy cream
Salt and ground black pepper
Fresh thyme leaves, to garnish
TO SERVE (OPTIONAL)
1½ cups wild mushrooms (ceps,
  chanterelles, pieds-de-mouton)
½ stock (4 tablespoons) unsalted
  butter

1. Wipe over the pheasant joints and remove any stray feathers.

2. Melt the butter in a saucepan and add the onion. Stir over the heat for 1–2 minutes and add the pheasant joints. Fry gently for about 10 minutes, till the meat seizes and takes a little color.

3. Add the wine and 1½ quarts water and bring to a boil. Turn down the heat. Add the bay leaf, thyme, and allspice. Season with salt and pepper. Cover loosely and simmer for 30–40 minutes, until the meat is tender. Strain the broth and pick out the bones, reserving the meat.

4. Return the broth to the pan. Add the chestnuts, reheat until boiling (add more water if necessary), and simmer for 30 minutes more, until the chestnuts are soft and floury. Mash a little to thicken the broth.

5. Meanwhile, shred the pheasant meat (or dice it finely) and return it to the soup. Stir in the cream, bubble up again, and ladle the soup into bowls.

6. Serve with the mushrooms, if using, cleaned, sliced and lightly sautéed in the butter. Sprinkle with the fresh thyme leaves.

SPANISH CHICKEN SOUP WITH CHICKPEAS

Spain's *cocidos*—the generic name for anything cooked in a boiling pot—have their origin in Moorish Andalusia, though the dish is now naturalized throughout the country. Each region has its own particular recipe, though these can change from household to household.

SERVES 4–6

1lb chickpeas, soaked overnight in water
½ head of garlic
Short length of ham bone or bacon knuckle
2 chicken quarters (a boiling fowl is best; a chicken will do)
6–8 black peppercorns
½ teaspoon coriander seeds
1 onion, roughly chopped
1 bay leaf and 1 marjoram sprig
1–2 large potatoes, cut into bite-sized pieces
1 generous handful of spinach or chard leaves, shredded
2 tablespoons olive oil
Salt and ground black pepper

1. Drain the chickpeas and put them in a saucepan with water to cover. Bring to a boil and skim off the gray foam that rises.

2. Hold the clump of garlic in a flame until the papery covering blackens at the edges and the air is filled with the fine scent of roasting garlic cloves. Drop it into the pan with the ham bone and chicken quarters. Add the peppercorns, coriander seeds, onion, bay leaf, and marjoram. Do not add salt. Bring to a boil and reduce the heat. Cover and cook for 1½–3 hours, or until the chickpeas are quite soft.

3. Keep the soup at a gentle bubble—don't let the temperature drop or add salt as this will toughen the skins of the chickpeas and they will never seem to soften. If you need to add water, make sure it is boiling.

4. Add the potatoes 30 minutes before the end of cooking and stir in the spinach or chard 10 minutes before the end. Just before you are ready to serve, season and stir in the olive oil.

CHICKEN GHIVETCH WITH RICE NOODLES

Ghivetch is the generic name for a thick soup, a Turkish word that spread throughout the Ottoman Empire. This is the Bulgarian version—a chicken soup finished with tomato, spiced with cinnamon, and fortified with any of the small, rice-shaped soup noodles popular in the Mediterranean.

SERVES 4–6

4 tablespoons olive oil
1 small onion, diced
3–4 garlic cloves, chopped
2ozs rice-shaped noodles
1lb plum tomatoes, skinned, seeded and diced (or use canned)
1 quart chicken stock (see page 16)
1–2 bay leaves
1 short cinnamon stick
1 tablespoon small soup noodles
Salt and ground black pepper

TO GARNISH

About 2ozs feta cheese, crumbled
1 tablespoon mint leaves

1. Heat the oil in a medium saucepan and fry the onion and garlic until softened and golden. Stir in the rice-shaped noodles and cook until the grains turn transparent, about 2–3 minutes.

2. Add the tomatoes and stir over the heat until they go mushy, about 2–3 minutes. Add the stock, bay leaves, and cinnamon. Bring to a boil, reduce the heat, and cover loosely. Cook gently for 20–30 minutes, or until the rice-shaped noodles are tender.

3. Stir in the soup noodles and cook for 5–10 minutes more. Taste and adjust the seasoning.

4. Ladle into soup bowls and garnish with crumbled feta cheese and a few mint leaves.

TIP
The traditional handmade soup pastas of Greece and Turkey, tarhonya, are still made in the villages by drying scraps of rolled or grated pasta dough, bound with yogurt or sour milk, in the sun—a convenient way of storing valuable milk-protein for the winter.

CHINESE HOT & SOUR CHICKEN BROTH

A warming, winter soup just as they like it in Szichuan, a mountainous region in the southwestern corner of China. Szichuan cooks are famous for both their skill and the fieriness of their food.

SERVES 4

1½ quarts chicken stock
   (see page 16)
2–3 dried chiles
1 tablespoon soy sauce
3–4 dried tree ear mushrooms
1 can bamboo shoots, drained and
   slivered
4ozs fresh firm tofu, diced
1 egg, forked to blend
2 tablespoons rice wine vinegar
   (or white wine vinegar)
1–2 spring onions, finely chopped
Salt and ground black pepper

1. In a large saucepan, bring the chicken stock to a boil and bubble it up until reduced to 1 quart of well-flavored broth. Strain through a sieve lined with a clean cloth. Return the broth to the pan with the chiles and soy sauce. Reheat until boiling and remove from the heat. Leave to infuse for 10 minutes, then remove and discard the chiles.

2. Meanwhile, set the mushrooms to soak in boiling water until they soften and double their size; remove the hard stalks and tear the caps into small pieces.

3. Add the mushrooms to the soup, return it to the heat and bring back to a boil. Reduce the heat and simmer for 10 minutes. Add the bamboo shoots and diced tofu, and reheat until boiling. Make a whirlpool in the middle and pour in the egg in a steady stream through the tines of a fork, keeping the pan on a boil so that the egg sets in delicate spidery strands. Stir in the vinegar, taste and adjust the seasoning. Place a little chopped onion into each soup bowl and ladle the broth over.

COLD ALMOND & CHICKEN VELOUTÉ

Freshly ground almonds add a subtle layer of flavor and texture to a classic French broth thickened with cream and egg yolk. This soup is delicious served with hot Melba toast.

SERVES 4–6

¾ cup blanched almonds
2½ cups chicken stock
  (see page 16)
1¾ cups light cream
2 egg yolks
TO SERVE
Light cream
Toasted flaked almonds

1. Put the almonds in a food processor with enough chicken stock to let the blades revolve freely, then process the almonds to a paste. Add the rest of the ingredients and continue to process until smooth.

2. Transfer the contents of the processor to a heavy saucepan. Heat gently without letting the soup boil, stirring continuously until the liquid thickens slightly—don't let it overcook. Cool and transfer to the refrigerator to chill.

3. Serve with an extra swirl of cream and a few toasted almond flakes.

TIP
To make Melba toast, take slices of thick-cut, day-old bread and toast them lightly on both sides. Trim off the crusts, then carefully slit each slice in two down the middle through the soft crumb. Dry the now thin slices in a medium oven (350°F) for 10 minutes until brittle and brown.

MEXICAN CHICKEN SOUP WITH CHILAQUILES

SERVES 4–6

1 quart chicken stock (see page 16)

1 chicken breast fillet, skinned

Oil for shallow frying

8 day-old cornmeal tortillas, sliced into fine strips

FOR THE ACCOMPANIMENTS

2–3 large ripe tomatoes, peeled, seeded, and diced

1 mild onion or 3–4 spring onions, finely chopped

1–2 avocados, stoned, peeled, and diced

A few cilantro or epazote sprigs or mint leaves, roughly chopped

Quartered limes, for squeezing

Puffy pork cracklings (*chicharrónes*)

Grated Cheddar-type cheese (*queso añejo*)

Pickled chiles (chipotles or moras)

1. Bring a stock to the boil in a large saucepan. Add the chicken breast and simmer for about 10 minutes, or until the meat is perfectly firm. Remove with a slotted spoon and shred thinly.

2. Meanwhile heat a finger's width of oil in a frying pan and fry the tortilla strips, a few at a time, until puffed and crisp. Transfer to paper towels to drain.

3. Provide everyone with a bowl and a spoon, and set the extras out on the table, along with the shredded chicken and the crisp tortilla strips (*chilaquiles*). Return the broth to a boil while everyone fills their bowls with whatever accompaniments they choose.

4. Ladle the broth into the bowls, warning everyone not to burn their tongues at the first sip. Some people like a squeeze of lime juice and a nibble of pickled chile.

TIP
Add the chicharrónes *after you've eaten some of the broth, as they soak up the broth and become wonderfully soft and glutinous.*

SCOTTISH COCK-A-LEEKIE

SERVES 4–6

4½lbs chicken wings and drumsticks
4½lbs leeks, weighed with their
  green tops
1 teaspoon sea salt
½ teaspoon peppercorns (white
  for preference)
1 short cinnamon stick
2 cloves
4–6 prunes (soaked or unsoaked)
Salt and ground black pepper
Chopped fresh parsley, to garnish

1. Rinse the chicken pieces and pack them in a large saucepan with 3 quarts water. Bring to a boil and skim off the gray foam that rises. Meanwhile, trim the leeks, saving the outer leaf trimmings and tops. Slice the remainder thinly, keeping the white and green parts in separate piles.

2. Add the leek trimmings and tops to the broth, return it to a boil, then add the sea salt, peppercorns, cinnamon, and cloves. Turn the heat to low, cover loosely, and leave to bubble gently for about 1 hour.

3. Remove the pan from the heat and tip everything into a sieve set over a bowl to catch the broth. Pick out the chicken meat and reserve, discarding the bones, skin and other debris.

4. Return the broth to the pan and bring back to a boil. Add the white part of the leeks and prunes to the broth. Return the pan to a boil, reduce the heat, cover loosely, and bubble gently for 30 minutes, or until the leeks are soft and almost melted into the broth. The broth should be reduced by one-third. If not, bubble it up until the volume is right. If it has lost too much volume, add some boiling water.

5. Cut the remaining leek greens into matchsticks and stir them into the broth. Return the reserved chicken to the broth.

6. Reheat until boiling and cook for 2–3 minutes to soften the leeks but keeping their brightness. Season and ladle into hot soup plates. Garnish with a generous sprinkling of parsley.

TURKISH CHICKEN & YOGURT SOUP WITH WALNUTS

SERVES 4–6

2 boned chicken thighs, skinned and
   sliced
1 quart chicken stock (see page 16)
$1/3$ cup walnut pieces
3 cups plain yogurt
1 egg yolk
Salt

TO GARNISH

1 small onion, finely sliced into
   half-moons
$1/4$ stick (2 tablespoons) butter
1 teaspoon dried mint (or
   2 teaspoons finely chopped
   fresh mint)

1. Put the chicken and stock in a medium saucepan and bring to a boil. Cover loosely and reduce the heat to a gentle simmer. Leave to cook for 30–40 minutes, or until the chicken is tender and the stock has reduced to 3 cups of well-flavored broth. Cool to finger temperature.

2. Meanwhile, grind the walnuts to a powder in a food processor or blender. Add the broth and chicken to the processor and process until well blended. Add the yogurt and the egg yolk, and process again. Return the soup to the pan and reheat very gently, whisking throughout, until just below boiling point. Simmer for 5 minutes, or until the soup has thickened a little. Taste and add salt if necessary.

3. Meanwhile, prepare the garnish: fry the onion in the butter until brown and beginning to blacken, then add the dried or fresh mint and remove from the heat.

4. Ladle the soup into bowls and garnish each portion with the buttery, mint-flavored onions.

POLISH CHICKEN SOUP

SERVES 4–6

2 quarts chicken stock (see page 16)
2–3 ribs celery, diced
1 large carrot, peeled and chunked
1 onion, chopped
1/2 teaspoon black peppercorns
FOR THE KREPLACH DOUGH
1 1/2 cups all-purpose flour
1/2 teaspoon salt
1 large egg
Chopped parsley, to garnish
FOR THE FILLING
1 tablespoon chicken fat or oil
1 small onion, finely chopped
1 cup finely chopped cooked chicken
   or ground raw chicken
1 tablespoon finely chopped
   fresh parsley
1 egg, forked to blend
Salt and ground black pepper

1. Put all the stock ingredients in a large saucepan and bring to the boil, then boil uncovered until reduced by half—about 30 minutes. Strain through a cloth-lined sieve and return to the pan.

2. Meanwhile, make the kreplach. In a large bowl, work the dough ingredients together until perfectly smooth and elastic (you may need more flour or a dash of water). Shape the dough into a ball, put it into a plastic bag and leave to rest while you prepare the filling.

3. For the filling, heat the fat or oil in a small pan and fry the onion gently until it turns transparent. Add the chicken and fry gently if raw—just mix in if cooked. Add the remaining filling ingredients and mix well. Season with salt and pepper.

4. Roll out the kreplach dough as thinly as you can and cut into squares about the size of your palm. To do this, roll the dough into a long thin bolster and cut into even segments.

5. Put a teaspoonful of the filling into the middle of each square, brush the edges with a little water and fold over the corners diagonally to make a triangle, pinching the edges to seal. Bring the long points together and pinch firmly to make a ring. Leave to rest for 15–20 minutes.

6. Bring the chicken broth back to a boil and slip in the kreplach a few at a time—keep the broth on a boil so the kreplach don't stick to the bottom of the pan. Boil for about 20 minutes, until the kreplachs come to the surface. Ladle into bowls and garnish with a generous sprinkle of chopped parsley.

INDONESIAN CHICKEN & COCONUT SOUP

SERVES 4–6

12ozs chicken breast fillet, skinned

2 tablespoons vegetable oil

1 medium onion, slivered vertically

2 garlic cloves, crushed

1 teaspoon ground coriander

1 teaspoon chile powder

1 teaspoon ground ginger

1 teaspoon ground turmeric

1 lime leaf or bay leaf

$1/2$ lemon grass stalk or 1 strip of
    lemon zest

2 tablespoons lime or lemon juice

$2^1/2$ cups coconut milk

2ozs cellophane noodles, soaked for
    10 minutes to swell

Salt

TO GARNISH

Leaves from a few mint sprigs

$1/2$ cucumber, peeled and cut into
    matchsticks

1. Cut the chicken into thin slivers, salt lightly, and set aside.

2. Heat the oil in a medium saucepan and fry the onion and garlic until they soften—don't let them brown. Stir in the spices, lime or bay leaf, and lemon grass or lemon zest. Add the lime or lemon juice and 1 tablespoon water. Bubble up, reduce the heat, and simmer for 10 minutes.

3. Remove the lemon grass or lemon zest and discard. Add the chicken and simmer for 5 minutes more, or until firm and opaque. Add the coconut milk and $1^1/4$ cups water and bubble up again. Stir in the noodles and bring back to a boil. Taste and add more salt if necessary.

4. Ladle into bowls and garnish with mint leaves and cucumber.

RABBIT SOUP WITH BEER & PRUNES

Beer soups, plain or fancy, are popular throughout all the brewing nations, but particularly among the Belgians, whose country has a reputation for excellence based on a strong tradition of monastic breweries. Here, tender hutch-reared rabbit flavors a beer-based broth sweetened with prunes.

SERVES 4–6

1lb rabbit meat, diced
2 tablespoons butter or oil
1 tablespoon diced bacon
1 large onion, diced
1 large carrot, diced
1 celeriac root, diced
1 teaspoon juniper berries, crushed
½ cup prunes, soaked for 4 hours
   to swell
2 cups lager (Belgian gueuze,
   for preference)
Salt and ground black pepper
Chopped spring onion, to garnish
TO SERVE
Rye bread
Radishes
Unsalted butter

1. Fry the rabbit meat in the butter or oil, in a medium saucepan until it stiffens and browns a little. Remove and reserve. Add the bacon, onion, and carrot, and fry gently until they take a little color.

2. Return the rabbit to the pan and add the diced celeriac, juniper berries, prunes, and beer. Bubble up until the steam no longer smells of alcohol. Add 1 quart water and return to a boil. Reduce the heat and cook gently, loosely covered, for 1 hour. Add more boiling water if necessary. Mash the vegetables a little to thicken the broth. Taste and adjust the seasoning.

3. Ladle into soup bowls and garnish with chopped spring onion. Serve with thickly sliced rye bread, crisp red radishes, and unsalted butter.

MEAT

AUSTRIAN BEEF BROTH WITH BACON & BUTTER DUMPLINGS

SERVES 4–6

FOR THE BROTH

2¼lbs shin of beef (tied in a piece)

2¼lbs smoked bacon (tied in a piece)

2–3 mature carrots, chopped

1 Hamburg parsley or a small parsnip, diced

1 small bunch of parsley, chopped

½ celeriac or 4 ribs celery, chopped

2 onions

2–3 garlic cloves

1 teaspoon ground allspice

½ teaspoon black peppercorns

FOR THE DUMPLINGS

½ stick (4 tablespoons) unsalted butter

1 egg, lightly forked to blend

¾ cup all-purpose flour

Salt

Chopped fresh parsley and chives, to garnish

1. Put all the broth ingredients in a large saucepan and pour in enough water to cover generously—about 3 quarts. Bring to a boil, skim off any gray foam that rises, then reduce the heat. Cover loosely and simmer gently for 2 hours, or until the meats are perfectly tender. Add more boiling water if necessary. (The water should just tremble, no more.)

2. Meanwhile, make the dumplings. In a warm bowl, beat the butter until creamy. Beat in the egg, then fold in the flour and a little salt. Beat well until you have a smooth paste. Cover and leave to rest for 30 minutes.

3. Remove the meats when they are quite soft and reserve. Strain out and discard the flavoring vegetables (for a good, clear broth, strain the stock through a sieve lined with a clean cloth). Boil the remaining broth until it reduces to about 1½ quarts.

4. Using a teaspoon and a clean wet finger, drop little blobs of the dumpling paste into the boiling broth. Turn down the heat to a gentle simmer and poach the dumplings for about 15 minutes, or until firm and light.

5. Ladle the broth and dumplings into hot bowls. Finish with slices of the reserved meat and a good sprinkle of chopped parsley and chives.

BEEF CONSOMMÉ

A crystal-clear beef consommé is one of the simplest and most delicious of starters. If you have a friendly butcher, get him to add a couple of sawn-up marrow bones to strengthen the flavor.

SERVES 6–8

2¼lbs lean shin of beef, chopped
2 large onions, unskinned and
   chopped
2 large carrots, chopped
2 quarts strained beef stock
   (see page 15)
1 tablespoon chopped tomato flesh,
   if necessary
3 egg whites, well whisked
Salt and ground black pepper

TIP
A wonderful addition to the consommé is marrow bones. Cover the open ends with foil to stop the marrow escaping during the cooking, and scoop out the marrow onto hot toast to serve as a nibble.

1. Put the beef in a large saucepan with the onions, carrots, and stock. Bring to a boil and leave to simmer gently for 2 hours, or until the meat has given up all its goodness and the broth has reduced by half. If the color is not sufficiently golden, you may add a tablespoon of chopped tomato flesh.

2. Strain the broth, discarding the vegetables and meat (or save it for a beef salad), and return the broth to the pan.

3. Bring the broth back to a boil and whisk in the egg whites. Return to a boil, reduce the heat, and simmer for 20 minutes, or until the egg whites float to the top, collecting all the impurities on the way.

4. Remove the pan from the heat and strain the broth through a sieve lined with a clean cloth. Blot the surface with paper towels to remove any lingering bubbles of fat.

5. Reheat, taste, and adjust the seasoning. Ladle into double-handled consommé bowls—very French.

CONSOMMÉ À L'INDIENNE

An elegant Anglo-Indian invention, easy and quick to make, which has its name from Lady Curzon, wife of a Viceroy of India in Queen Victoria's day. Simple but surprisingly good, particularly with poppadoms on the side.

SERVES 4–6

2¹/₂ cups beef consommé
  (see page 78)
2–3 cardamom pods, toasted and
  crushed
1–2 small dried chiles
TO GARNISH
²/₃ cup heavy cream, whipped
1 teaspoon curry powder

1. Bring the consommé to a boil in a large saucepan with the cardamom pods and chiles. Remove from the heat and leave to infuse for 10 minutes.
2. Strain, ladle into small soup bowls, and top each serving with a spoonful of whipped cream and a pinch of curry powder.

TIP
Emphasize the historic connection by serving it with a selection of small Indian snacks such as crisp little samosas— spicy vegetable fritters.

SCOTCH BROTH WITH LAMB & BARLEY

A well-flavored broth made with bony chunks of lamb and fortified with vegetables and barley. Scotch broth, whether it's a soup or a stew, depends on how much liquid is added. Traditionally it is served as the main course of a family meal.

SERVES 4–6

½ cup pearl barley, soaked for
   3–4 hours to swell
2¼lbs neck of lamb, chunked
1–2 bay leaves
2¼lbs potatoes, diced
2 large carrots, diced
2 good-sized leeks, sliced (save
   the best of the trimmings)
1 large yellow turnip, diced
Salt and cracked peppercorns
Chopped fresh parsley, to garnish

1. Strain the barley, reserving the soaking water. Make up the volume of water to 2 quarts. Put the meat into a large flameproof casserole with the barley and the water. Season with salt and cracked peppercorns. Add the bay leaves, bring to a boil, and reduce the heat. Cover and leave to simmer gently for 1 hour, or until the meat is dropping off the bone. After the first 30 minutes, add the vegetables and more boiling water, if needed.

2. When the meat is soft enough to eat with a spoon and the vegetables have almost collapsed into the broth, it's ready.

3. Ladle into bowls and finish with finely shredded leek trimmings and chopped parsley.

STEAK SOUP

A winter soup thickened with flour and fortified with ground beef, just as they like it on the rolling plains of Kansas.

SERVES 4–6

⅓ cup butter
3 tablespoons all-purpose flour
1½ quarts beef stock (see page 15)
1 large onion, diced
1 large carrot, diced
2 cups corn kernels
1¼ cups red wine
2 tablespoons red wine vinegar
2 tablespoons tomato paste
1 tablespoon Worcestershire sauce
1lb steak (use ground lean beef)
Salt and ground black pepper
2 tablespoons chopped parsley,
   to garnish

1. Melt all but 1 tablespoon of the butter in a large saucepan and stir in the flour. Fry gently for 2–3 minutes, or until it turns golden and takes a little color—don't let it burn. Slowly add the beef stock, stirring or whisking continuously until smooth, then bubble up until it no longer smells of raw flour, about 10 minutes.

2. Add the vegetables, wine, vinegar, and tomato paste, with the Worcestershire sauce and seasonings. Return to a boil, reduce the heat, and simmer for 30 minutes, or until the vegetables are soft.

3. Meanwhile, fry the minced steak in the remaining butter until brown, turning it with a spatula to avoid large lumps. Stir the meat into the soup and simmer for 15 minutes more to marry the flavors.

4. Ladle into warm bowls and garnish with plenty of chopped parsley before serving.

HUNGARIAN LAMB SOUP WITH PAPRIKA & CREAM

A Hungarian *gulyas*—the Magyar name for a soup—is traditionally cooked in a heavy iron pot suspended over an open fire in the yard; a custom that still survives in the villages. In the olden days, the meat was a leathery hank of air-dried beef or horsemeat: the staple diet of the Masgyar herdsmen who settled the banks of the Danube.

SERVES 4—6

1lb stewing lamb, finely diced
2 medium onions, thinly sliced
2 large carrots, diced
1 celeriac root, diced
Hamburg parsley or 1 small bunch of
    Italian parsley, finely chopped
1 teaspoon allspice berries, crushed
2 heaped tablespoons mild paprika
1 teaspoon hot paprika or chile
    powder
Salt and ground black pepper
TO GARNISH (OPTIONAL)
$^2/_3$ cup sour cream
1 tablespoon chopped fresh
    marjoram

1. Put all the ingredients in a medium saucepan with $1^1/_2$ quarts cold water. Bring to a boil and reduce the heat. Cover and simmer gently until everything is tender and the soup is well flavored, about 30 minutes. Add more boiling water as necessary to maintain the volume while the soup is cooking.

2. Ladle into soup bowls and garnish each portion with a spoonful of sour cream and a pinch of chopped marjoram, if liked.

TRINIDADIAN PEPPERPOT

The traditional pepperpot, basically an all meat *pot au feu*, is seasoned with chile, sugar, and vinegar, and left to simmer quietly on the back burner of the stove for weeks, even months.

SERVES 4–6

1lb stewing beef, cubed

$^1/_2$lb diced pork belly, including the skin

2–3 chicken joints, chopped into bite-sized pieces

2 large onions, thickly sliced

1 Scotch Bonnet chile, seeded and chopped

1 short cinnamon stick

3–4 cloves

1 level teaspoon allspice berries, crushed

About 1 tablespoon vinegar

About 2 tablespoons dark brown sugar

1lb sweet potato, diced

$^1/_2$lb callaloo greens or spinach, shredded

TO SERVE

Pickled chiles

Quartered limes

1. Put all the ingredients except the sweet potato and greens into a flameproof casserole. Add enough water to cover everything generously— at least 1 quart. Bring to a boil, reduce the heat and cover tightly. Simmer for 1$^1/_2$–2 hours. Alternatively, transfer the casserole to the oven and cook at 300°F.

2. Add the diced sweet potato and cook for 1–1$^1/_2$ hours more until the meat is perfectly tender and the cooking juices well reduced. Or you can cook the sweet potato separately and add it at the end of cooking.

3. Dilute the pepperpot juices with enough boiling water to return the soup to its original volume. Reheat and stir in the shredded greens, bubble up for 5 minutes, or until the leaves soften and collapse. Taste and adjust the seasoning with a little more sugar or a touch more vinegar, if needed.

4. Ladle into bowls and serve with pickled chiles and quartered limes.

TIP
Trinidadians would keep the basic broth going for years, restoring the volume of liquid with water as the broth is consumed, and adding more meat or fowl as and when available.

ANDALUSIAN OXTAIL SOUP

SERVES 4–6

1 whole oxtail, cut into its sections
2 tablespoons olive oil
¼lb serrano ham scraps, diced
4 garlic cloves, crushed
1–2 ribs celery, diced
1 carrot, diced
1lb tomatoes, skinned, seeded, and
    chopped (or use tinned)
½ cup white beans, soaked overnight
    and drained
1 tablespoon pimentón (Spanish
    paprika)
1 short cinnamon stick
3–4 cloves
½ teaspoon crushed black
    peppercorns
1 bay leaf
1¼ cups rough red wine
Salt and ground black pepper
Chopped fresh marjoram, to garnish

1. Wipe and trim the excess fat from the oxtail. Heat the oil in a large flameproof casserole or saucepan that will comfortably accommodate all the pieces. Turn the oxtail in the hot oil. Remove, reserve, and replace with the diced ham, garlic, celery, and carrot, and fry gently until the vegetables soften. Add the tomatoes and bubble up.

2. Return the oxtail to the casserole with the soaked beans. Add the spices and bay leaf with the wine and bubble up. Add 1½ quarts water—enough to submerge everything generously—and bring back to a boil. Cover tightly and leave to simmer on a very low heat for 3–4 hours, or until the meat is falling off the bones. Alternatively, cook in the oven at 300°F. Check from time to time and add more boiling water to maintain the volume. Taste and adjust the seasoning.

3. Pick the meat off the bones and discard the bones. Skim the excess golden fat from the soup (reserve for other purposes) and return the meat to the pan. Ladle into bowls and garnish with chopped marjoram.

GREEK LAMB SOUP WITH CINNAMON & QUINCE

A sweet-and-sour lamb soup in the Middle Eastern tradition: flavored with cinnamon and cloves, sweetened with prunes, soured with lemon juice, and finished with little cubes of quince. If you can't get quince use apple.

SERVES 4–6

1lb stewing lamb, trimmed and diced
2 tablespoons oil
1lb pickling onions, skinned and quartered
1 cup prunes, stoned or not, as you please
1 cup cooked chickpeas, drained
3–4 cloves (stick them into an onion quarter for ease of retrieval)
1 short cinnamon stick
1½ quarts beef, chicken, or vegetable stock (see pages 15 and 16) or water
Juice of 1 lemon
1 ripe quince or 2 yellow-fleshed apples, peeled and diced
Salt and ground black pepper

TO GARNISH (OPTIONAL)
2 tablespoons toasted flaked almonds
2 tablespoons pomegranate seeds

1. Rinse the meat and pat it dry. Heat the oil in a medium saucepan and fry the onions gently, shaking the pan over the heat until they take color. Push the onions to one side and fry the meat until it firms and browns a little, about 5 minutes.

2. Add the prunes, chickpeas, and spices with the stock or water. Bubble up, reduce the heat, and cover loosely. Leave to simmer gently for 1 hour, or until the meat is tender and the broth is well flavored.

3. Taste and season with salt and pepper. Add enough lemon juice to sharpen the flavor. Fold in the diced quince or apple. Bring back to a boil and simmer until the fruit is soft, about 5–10 minutes (don't let it collapse completely). You may need to add a little boiling water to keep the volume.

4. Ladle the soup into bowls and garnish, if you like, with a sprinkle of toasted almonds and a few pomegranate seeds.

PORK & VEGETABLE SOUP WITH DUMPLINGS

SERVES 4–6

½lb stewing pork, diced finely

1 tablespoon vegetable oil

1 onion, slivered

2 garlic cloves, crushed

1 large carrot, diced

1 parsnip, diced

1lb young turnips (reserve the green tops, if any), diced

1 teaspoon caraway seeds

Salt and ground black pepper

Chopped fresh dill, to garnish

FOR THE DUMPLINGS

1 egg

½ teaspoon salt

About ¾ cup all-purpose flour

TO SERVE

Pickled cucumbers

Black bread

1. Fry the meat in the oil in a medium saucepan. Let it brown a little, then add the onions and garlic. Let everything fry gently for 10 minutes, then add the carrot, parsnip, and turnips. Fry for 5 minutes more. Sprinkle with caraway seeds, season with salt, and add 1½ quarats water. Bring everything to a boil and reduce the heat. Cover and simmer for 30–40 minutes, or until the meat and vegetables are tender. Taste and season, if required.

2. Meanwhile, prepare the dumplings. Fork up the egg with the salt and work in enough flour to make a soft dough. Knead until it forms a smooth ball, cover with plastic wrap, and set it aside.

3. When you are ready to serve, bring a pan of salted water to a boil. Break off small pieces of the dough between your finger and thumb, pressing so that the dough is flattened into a little round cap. Toss the dumplings into the water a few at a time. They are ready as soon they bob to the surface. Transfer them to the soup pan with a slotted spoon. Continue until all are cooked.

4. Finely shred the turnip greens (if available). Reheat the soup and stir in the greens. Bubble up again and cook for 5 minutes, or until the greens are soft. Ladle into bowls and garnish with chopped dill. Serve with pickled cucumbers and black bread.

IRISH BACON & CABBAGE SOUP

All Irish soups and stews were traditionally cooked in the bastable—a three-toed iron cooking pot set at the edge of the peat fire and left on the hearth to simmer all day.

SERVES 4–6

3lbs bacon hock (including the bone and skin), well soaked
$\frac{1}{2}$ teaspoon black peppercorns
2–3 cloves
1 bay leaf
1lb onions, thinly sliced (save the skins for the broth)
2$\frac{1}{4}$lbs potatoes, sliced
2$\frac{1}{4}$lbs cabbage, shredded
4 tablespoons chopped fresh parsley
Salt and ground black pepper
Pitcher of melted butter (allow $\frac{1}{4}$ stick [2 tablespoons] per person), to serve (optional)

1. Put the bacon in a large saucepan with 2 quarts water. Bring to a boil and skim off the foam that rises. Taste the water; if it's very salty, drain it off, then cover with fresh water and proceed as before. Add the peppercorns, cloves, bay leaf, and onion skins (good for color in the broth). Reduce the heat, cover loosely, and simmer for 1–1$\frac{1}{2}$ hours, or until the broth is reduced by one third and the meat is perfectly tender.

2. Remove the bacon and carefully lift the meat off the bone. Carve into bite-sized pieces and reserve. Strain the broth and reserve.

3. Layer the onions, potatoes, and cabbage into the pan and cover with the bacon liquor. Bring to a boil and reduce the heat. Cover and simmer for 20–30 minutes, or until the vegetables are soft.

4. Return the meat to the pan and baste it with hot broth.

5. To serve, ladle the soup through the layers, making sure everyone gets their share of all elements. Sprinkle with the chopped parsley and season with salt and pepper. Serve with a pitcher of melted butter, if liked. This soup is also good with potatoes cooked in their jackets in a closed pot.

BEEF & PUMPKIN SOUP WITH NOODLES

A peppery, golden soup from sunny Madeira, Portugal's largest offshore island, made with the sweet-fleshed vegetables that thrive in the semi-tropical climate.

SERVES 4–6

12ozs stewing veal or shin of beef, finely diced

1 large onion, thinly sliced

¼ stick (2 tablespoons) butter

1lb plum tomatoes, peeled, seeded, and diced (or use tinned)

2¼lbs pumpkin flesh, diced

1lb sweet potato, diced

1–2 fresh red chiles (malagueta, for preference), seeded and chopped

2ozs vermicelli

Salt and ground black pepper

Salsa piri-piri or other chile sauce, to serve

1. Put the meat and onion in a large flameproof casserole with the butter, and fry gently until the meat and vegetables take a little color. Add the tomatoes and bubble up until the flesh collapses a little, mashing them with a spoon. Add the pumpkin and sweet potato. Bubble up again, reduce the heat and cover tightly. Cook gently for about 20 minutes.

2. Pour in 2½ cups water—enough to cover the vegetables generously. Reduce the heat, add the chiles and season with salt. Cover tightly with a lid and simmer gently for 20 minutes, or until the vegetables have softened but not quite collapsed. Add another 2½ cups boiling water and stir in the vermicelli. Cook for 5 minutes more, or until the noodles are perfectly tender. Taste and adjust the seasoning.

3. Ladle into bowls and hand round the salsa piri-piri or other chile sauce separately.

JAPANESE SHABU SHABU

SERVES 4–6

FOR THE MEAT AND VEGETABLES
1¼lbs tender beef sirloin, thinly slivered

½lbs dried shiitake mushrooms, soaked in water for 30 minutes to swell, trimmed and sliced

3 clusters enokitake mushrooms, divided into 3- or 4-stalk bunches

1 cabbage heart, shredded

12 spring onions

½lb firm tofu, cut into bite-sized cubes

FOR THE BROTH
About 2 quarts dashi or chicken stock (see pages 15 and 16)

1 small glass sake or other rice wine

2 tablespoons sugar

FOR THE DIPPING SAUCE
½ cup tahini

½ cup rice-wine vinegar

½ cup soy sauce

½ cup water

6 tablespoons lemon juice

FOR THE ACCOMPANIMENTS
Plain-cooked sticky white rice (½lb uncooked weight)

Pickled cucumbers or vegetables, diced

1. Set out the meat and vegetables on a large serving dish and place this on your dining table.

2. Bring the broth ingredients to a boil in a suitable cooking vessel— in Japan, an earthenware *donabe*—and keep the stock at a rolling boil in the middle of the table throughout the meal.

3. Mix the dipping sauce ingredients together until well blended and provide each person with their own small bowlful. Set out the accompaniments so that each diner can select their own combination.

4. Provide each person with a bowl of sticky rice, a spoon, and chopsticks, and give easy access to the accompaniments as well as the meat and vegetables. You can now serve the soup in one of two ways: tip a batch of meat and vegetables into the boiling soup and leave to cook for 3 minutes, then distribute the cooked food among your guests' bowls with a slotted spoon, or follow tradition and let each person help themselves with chopsticks, dipping the food into the broth and sauce, holding the bowl beneath to catch the drips.

5. The soup should be ladled into the empty rice bowls and drunk last, when it will be rich with accumulated deliciousness.

AUSTRIAN HAM BROTH WITH PANCAKE NOODLES

SERVES 4–6

1 quart ham, beef, or chicken stock
(see pages 15 and 16)
4 tablespoons diced ham
2 tablespoons chopped fresh parsley
1/2 teaspoon ground allspice
2 heaped tablespoons chopped fresh
parsley, to garnish
FOR THE PANCAKES
3 eggs
2 cups all-purpose flour
1/2 teaspoon salt
1 cup milk
About 1/2 stick (4 tablespoons)
unsalted butter
TO SERVE
Rye bread
Unsalted butter
Radishes

1. Put the stock in a large pan with the ham, parsley, and allspice. Bring to a boil and simmer while you make the pancakes.

2. Whisk the eggs with the flour and salt, and slowly add the milk until you have a smooth lump-free cream. Or drop everything in a food processor and process to blend.

3. Heat a small frying pan—whatever you use to cook omelets (or pancakes). Drop in a nugget of butter, wait until it melts, then roll it around the base of the pan. Pour in a tablespoonful of pancake batter and tip it around until it forms a thin layer. When the top surface is dry and the underside is browned (no more than 2–3 minutes), flip it over and cook the other side. Transfer to a folded cloth to keep it soft and warm. Continue until all the batter is used up.

4. When you are ready to serve, roll the pancakes up like little carpets and slice them right through to make narrow ribbons, like tagliatelle.

5. Ladle the boiling broth into warm soup bowls and divide the pancake ribbons among the bowls—or hand round separately for people to add their own. Garnish with the parsley. Rye bread with unsalted butter and radishes are good accompaniments.

JAMBALAYA WITH SPARE RIBS & OKRA

This soupy rice dish, eaten with a spoon from a bowl, belongs to the Louisiana tradition of Creole cooking. Possible inclusions are oysters, shrimp, crab, and chicken, although pork, in one form or another, is always included, along with okra, which gives the broth its characteristic gumminess.

SERVES 4–6

3–4 tablespoons oil
1lb pork spare ribs, cut into
   bite-sized chunks
2 tablespoons diced smoked ham
2 ribs celery, chopped
1 large onion, finely chopped
2 garlic cloves, chopped
1 green pepper, seeded and chopped
¼lb okra, trimmed
1lb peeled and diced tomatoes
   (or use canned)
1 cup round-grain rice
½ teaspoon dried oregano
½ teaspoon dried sage
4 cups chicken stock (see page 16)
   or water
Salt and ground black pepper
Louisiana hot sauce or Tabasco sauce,
   to serve

1. Heat 2 tablespoons of the oil in a flameproof enamel or earthenware casserole and fry the spare ribs, seasoning with salt and pepper as the meat browns. Remove the ribs and set aside.

2. Add the remaining oil and fry the ham, celery, onion, garlic, and green pepper gently until soft—don't let anything burn. Add the okra and let it fry for a couple of minutes. Add the tomatoes and bubble up again, mashing them to soften.

3. Return the spare ribs to the casserole and stir in the rice. Add the herbs and the stock or water. Bubble up, then reduce the heat. Cover loosely and simmer for about 20 minutes, or until the rice is tender—add more water if necessary.

4. Check the seasoning and ladle into bowls. Hand round a bottle of Louisiana hot sauce or Tabasco separately as appetites for chile vary.

SWEET-AND-SOUR PORK & CABBAGE SOUP

The broth for this unusual soup, a specialty of the one-time Saxon villages of northern Romania, is lightly thickened with egg and cream, sharpened with vinegar, and given a touch of sweetness with fresh grapes. In winter, it's made with smoked bacon and sweetened with raisins.

SERVES 4–6

½lb pork belly (including the skin), diced
1 tablespoon oil or 2 tablespoons lard
2 onions, diced
2 green peppers, seeded and diced
1lb green cabbage, shredded
2 tablespoons chopped fresh dill
2 tablespoons chopped fresh savory or tarragon
2 egg yolks
⅔ cup heavy cream
1 tablespoon wine vinegar
Salt and ground black pepper
2–3 tablespoons small white grapes, halved and seeded, to garnish

1. In a medium saucepan, fry the diced pork in the oil or lard until the meat begins to brown. Push it aside and add the onions and diced peppers. Season with salt and pepper and fry gently until golden, about 10 minutes. Add the cabbage and herbs, turning to blend. Pour in 1½ quarts boiling water. Bubble up and reduce the heat. Cover and cook gently for 20–30 minutes, or until the meat is tender and the cabbage soft. Remove the pan from the heat.

2. Meanwhile, in a small bowl, whisk the egg yolks with the cream and vinegar. Whisk in a ladleful of the hot broth and stir the mixture back into the soup. Gently reheat, stirring, until it thickens a little—don't let it boil.

3. Ladle into bowls and garnish each portion with a few halved grapes, peeled or not, as you please.

BEEF & CARROT SOUP WITH PARSNIP RIBBONS

SERVES 4–6

1 quart beef stock (see page 15)
2–3 short lengths of marrow bone
    or 1lb osso bucco (veal shin)
1lb large carrots, chopped
1 medium potato, diced
1 medium onion, diced
¼ stick (2 tablespoons) butter
1 tablespoon wine vinegar
½ teaspoon freshly grated nutmeg
Salt and ground black pepper

FOR THE PARSNIP RIBBONS

1 parsnip
Oil, for shallow frying

TO SERVE

Toast
Sea salt
Chopped fresh parsley

1. In a large saucepan, bring the beef stock to a boil with the marrow bone or osso bucco. Reduce the heat and leave to simmer for 30–40 minutes, or until reduced by one-third. Strain the broth and return it to the pan, reserving the marrow from the bones, if using. (If osso bucco was your choice, save the meat for a pasty, or shred, toss with a mustardy vinaigrette and serve with new potatoes.)

2. Bring the broth back to a boil with the carrots and potato. Reduce the heat and simmer for about 20 minutes, or until the vegetables are perfectly tender. Meanwhile, fry the onion gently in the butter in a small pan. Tip the contents of both pans into a food processor and process until smooth.

3. For the garnish, slice the parsnip into ribbons using a potato peeler. In a small frying pan, heat enough oil to submerge the ribbons and fry them, a few at a time, until crisp.

4. Return the soup to the pan, reheat until boiling, then stir in the vinegar. Add the nutmeg. Taste and adjust the seasoning.

5. Ladle into warm bowls and garnish each serving with a little tangle of parsnip ribbons and a sprinkling of freshly ground pepper, if liked.

6. Scoop the beef marrow, if available, onto crisp little rounds of toast. Sprinkle with a few grains of sea salt and chopped fresh parsley and serve it on the side.

FRENCH POT AU FEU

SERVES 4–6

2¼lbs beef rib or skirt, rolled and tied

2¼lbs beef shin, chunked and tied

1 knucklebone or marrow bone, chunked

2 medium onions, unskinned and quartered

1 small celery head, chopped

1–2 bay leaves

½ teaspoon black peppercorns

2–3 large carrots, chunked (save the trimmings)

2–3 large leeks, chunked (save the trimmings)

3–4 large potatoes, chunked

1 small firm, green cabbage (Savoy)

Salt and ground black pepper

TO SERVE

Aïoli (garlic mayonnaise)

Radishes

Capers

Cornichons

Bread

1. Put all the beef into a large saucepan. Cover with 3 quarts cold water. Bring to a boil and skim off the foam. Add the onions, celery, bay leaves, peppercorns, and trimmings from the carrots and leeks. Return the pan to a boil, then reduce the heat. Cover loosely and simmer gently for 2–3 hours, or until the meat is tender and the broth is reduced by one-third.

2. Strain the broth, discarding the trimmings and vegetables and reserving the meat. Remove the fat from the broth: either leave it to cool overnight, then lift off the solid layer of fat, or carefully skim off the fat with a spoon while the broth is still hot.

3. Reheat the broth and add the carrots and leeks. Bubble up, reduce the heat, and cook for 10 minutes. Add the potatoes and bubble up again. Reduce the heat and cook for 10 minutes more. Core the cabbage and slice it through the heart, creating a fan shape with the leaves joined at the base. Add to the pan. Bubble up again and cook for 10 minutes more, or until all the vegetables are tender. Check the seasoning.

4. Slice the meat so that everyone gets a share and reheat it with a ladleful of hot broth. Ladle the remainder of the broth and vegetables into warm soup plates and place the meat on top.

5. Hand round the aïoli, along with side dishes of radishes, capers, cornichons and plenty of bread for mopping. You'll also need a carafe of cheap red wine to enable your guests to *faire chabrot*—a gesture of appreciation made by pouring the wine into the last ladleful of hot soup and drinking it directly from the bowl.

VEGETABLES

CLEAR BEET CONSOMMÉ

A sophisticated version of the robust Russian borscht, this is a delicate, ruby-red consommé as served at London's famous Mirabelle restaurant in the postwar years.

SERVES 4–6

1 quart strong vegetable stock
   (see page 16) or beef or chicken
   consommé (see pages 15 and 16),
   if preferred
1 large beet, cooked and grated
²⁄₃ cup thick, drained yogurt
   (Greek style)
A few dill sprigs, to garnish

1. Heat the consommé with the grated beet in a saucepan and remove the pan from the heat as soon as it boils.

2. Strain, discarding the beet, which should have tinted the soup a deep ruby-pink.

3. Reheat the consommé and ladle into small bowls. Drop a spoonful of yogurt into each bowl and garnish with a sprig of dill.

CHESTNUT & CELERIAC SOUP WITH CINNAMON

A thick, nourishing winter soup from the wooded uplands of Bulgaria. The celeriac delivers a robust earthiness that perfectly balances the natural sweetness of the chestnuts.

SERVES 4–6

12ozs fresh unskinned chestnuts
1lb celeriac, diced
3 cups vegetable or chicken stock
   (see page 16), if preferred
1 short cinnamon stick
2 egg yolks, forked to blend
½ stick (4 tablespoons) butter,
   chopped into small pieces
Salt and ground black pepper
1–2 teaspoons ground cinnamon,
   to garnish

TIP
*The soup is traditionally
made in winter with dried
chestnuts milled to flour,
and with fresh nuts
in fall.*

1. Prick the chestnuts in one or two places with a fork or the point of a knife and drop them into a saucepan with enough cold water to cover. Bring to a boil and cook the chestnuts in their jackets for about 15 minutes. Drain and transfer to a bowl of cold water to loosen the skins. Remove both the tough outer shell and the russet inner skin.

2. Put the peeled chestnuts back into the pan with the diced celeriac, the chicken or vegetable stock, and the cinnamon stick. Bring to a boil, reduce the heat, and simmer for 30–40 minutes, or until the chestnuts are perfectly soft.

3. Remove the cinnamon stick and reserve a few of the whole chestnuts.

4. Push everything else through a sieve or transfer to a food processor and process until smooth.

5. Return the soup to the pan, taste, and add salt and freshly ground pepper. Whisk in the egg yolks and the butter. Reheat carefully without letting the soup reboil.

6. Serve the soup in bowls, garnishing each portion with the reserved whole chestnuts and a sprinkle of the ground cinnamon.

CURRIED PARSNIP SOUP

The subtlety of garam masala, the basic curry blend of the Indian kitchen, highlights the sweetness and earthiness of a creamy parsnip soup.

SERVES 4–6

2¼lbs parsnips, chunked
1 quart vegetable stock (see page 16)
1 tablespoon garam masala
Salt and ground black pepper
TO GARNISH
1 onion, thinly sliced into half moons
¼ stick (2 tablespoons) butter
A few cardamom seeds

1. Put the parsnips and stock in a large saucepan and cook until perfectly tender—allow 20–30 minutes.

2. Drop the parsnips with their cooking liquor into a food processor and process until smooth. Add the garam masala and dilute with a little boiling water if it's too thick or if you have more people to feed. Check the seasoning and reheat until just boiling.

3. Meanwhile, prepare the garnish. Fry the onion gently in the butter in a small frying pan. After 5 minutes, add the crushed cardamom seeds and continue to fry until the onion is golden and perfectly soft, allowing 10–15 minutes.

4. Ladle the soup into warmed soup bowls and garnish with a swirl of cardamom-flavored fried onion.

JAPANESE MISO SOUP WITH SHIITAKE MUSHROOMS

Miso soup is based on dashi stock, a simple, nutritious broth made with dried bonito flakes and a pre-prepared seaweed. All the ingredients are widely available in oriental foodstores.

SERVES 4–6

1 quart dashi stock (see page 15)
¼ cup dried shiitake mushrooms, soaked in hot water for 30 minutes to swell
5 tablespoons miso paste
2 tablespoons dried wakame (seaweed) flakes
1–2 cilantro sprigs, leaves only, to garnish

TIP
For a more substantial soup, add a spoonful of diced beancurd (tofu) to each serving.

1. Heat the dashi stock in a large saucepan until boiling. Meanwhile, drain the shiitake mushrooms, remove and discard the tough stalks, and slice the caps.

2. As soon as the stock boils, remove a ladleful and stir it into the miso paste, mixing until well blended, and then stir it back into the stock.

3. Return the stock to a boil. Add the mushrooms and wakame flakes, then simmer gently for 10–15 minutes, or until the mushrooms are tender and the soup has taken their flavor.

4. Ladle into warm bowls (Japanese soup bowls are lidded for extra drama when serving), garnishing each portion with cilantro leaves.

FRENCH ONION SOUP

A clear onion soup served with thick slices of baguette topped with cheese and toasted is one of the great dishes of the French bourgeois kitchen. A deep, round-bellied earthenware casserole, the *marmite*, is the traditional cooking pot.

SERVES 4–6

1½lbs onions, very thinly sliced
   in rings
⅓ cup butter
⅔ cup white wine
3 cups vegetable stock (see page 16)
   or beef stock (see page 15),
   if preferred
Salt and ground black pepper
TO SERVE
4–6 thick slices of day-old baguette,
   cut on the slant
About 1 cup grated cheese

1. In a large saucepan, gently fry the onions in the butter, stirring every now and then, for at least 20 minutes, or until they are soft and golden. Add the wine and stock and season with salt and pepper. Bring back to a boil and reduce the heat. Leave to simmer for about 20 minutes—longer if more convenient.

2. Meanwhile, preheat the oven to 300°F. Put the baguette slices on a baking sheet in the oven and leave to dry.

3. Divide the slices among the soup bowls, then ladle in the hot soup. The bread slices will rise to the top. Either sprinkle the cheese onto the bread and slip the bowls under the broiler to melt and brown the cheese, or hand round the cheese for people to add their own. Alternatively, serve the bread on the side.

WATERCRESS, LEEK, & POTATO SOUP

With this soup, a plain, stock-based liquor thickened with potato, and flavored with leek, provides a gentle background for the pepperiness of the watercress.

SERVES 4–6

1 large bunch of watercress
1 large potato, diced
1 large leek, diced
3 cups vegetable or chicken stock (see page 16), if preferred
½ stick (4 tablespoons) unsalted butter, cut into small pieces
½ teaspoon freshly grated nutmeg
Salt and ground black pepper
⅔ cup sour cream, to garnish

1. Trim the watercress leaves from the stalks. Reserve the leaves and put the stalks in a medium saucepan with the potato and leek. Add the stock and bring to a boil. Reduce the heat to a simmer, cover loosely, and cook for 20 minutes, or until the potato is perfectly soft.

2. Transfer the contents of the pan to a food processor and process until smooth. Add the watercress leaves (reserve a few for garnishing) and process briefly again.

3. Return the soup to the pan and reheat until just boiling. Taste, then season with salt, pepper, and nutmeg. Swirl in some sour cream and garnish with the watercress leaves before serving.

CARROT & FRESH GINGER SOUP

The sweetness of the carrots is balanced by the fieriness of ginger and sharpness of vinegar—a simple winter soup with clear, clean flavors.

SERVES 4

2¼lbs carrots, sliced
1 potato, diced
1 teaspoon grated fresh ginger root
1 tablespoon cider or white wine
   vinegar
Salt and ground black pepper
1 small handful of fresh cilantro,
   roughly torn, to garnish

1. Put the carrots in a saucepan and add the potato and ginger. Add 3 cups water and cook until the vegetables are perfectly soft. Put everything into the food processor and process until smooth and thick—dilute with boiling water if necessary. Add the vinegar, taste, and season with salt and pepper.

2. Ladle the soup into warm bowls and garnish each portion with a few cilantro leaves.

CORN CHOWDER

This simple, creamy corn soup is finished with tomato and basil, as they like it in Chile. Serve with cornmeal tortillas or Chilean *arepas*—they're thicker, paler, and softer than the more familiar Mexican flatbread.

SERVES 4–6

2 cups fresh corn kernels
1 cup light cream
1¼ cups milk
Salt and ground black pepper
TO GARNISH
1 large ripe tomato, peeled, seeded, and diced
1 tablespoon fresh basil leaves, shredded
Sliced fresh red chile or chile flakes
TO SERVE
Quartered limes
Tabasco sauce

1. Put the corn kernels in a medium saucepan with 1¾ cups water (no salt). Bring to a boil, turn down the heat, and cook for 10 minutes, or until the corn is tender and the cooking liquid has thickened with the starch. Remove 2 tablespoons of the corn with a slotted spoon and reserve.

2. Put the remainder of the corn and the cooking liquor into a blender with the cream and milk, and process until well blended. Taste and season lightly with salt and pepper.

3. Return the soup to the pan and reheat gently, stirring continuously, until just boiling. Stir in the reserved corn kernels and diced tomato.

4. Ladle the soup into warm soup bowls and garnish with shredded basil leaves and slivers of fresh chile or a few chile flakes.

5. To serve, hand round the limes and Tabasco sauce for people to add what they like.

HERB SOUP WITH CHERVIL

A fresh-flavored, spring soup popular throughout Germany, but particularly in Bavaria, which is traditionally served on Easter Thursday—the day when church-going households scrubbed and painted their houses inside and out ready for Holy Friday.

SERVES 4–6

4ozs chervil
7ozs other salad herbs (such as dandelion, mâche, watercress, parsley, tarragon, and chicory)
½ stick (4 tablespoons) butter
1 large onion, finely chopped
1 large potato, diced
Salt and ground black pepper

1. Pick over and wash the herbs, stripping the leaves from those stalks that are too woody.

2. Melt the butter in a large saucepan and fry the onion gently until transparent. Add the herbs and stir them over the heat for 2–3 minutes, until they collapse.

3. Add the diced potato and 3 cups water. Bring to a boil and then reduce the heat. Simmer for 20 minutes. Mash the potato into the soup to thicken it a little. Taste and add salt and freshly ground pepper.

4. Ladle the soup into warm bowls and serve.

TIP
The dominant flavoring in the soup should be chervil, also known as Sweet Cecily, a licorice-flavored herb with good digestive properties. Tarragon, a member of the same botanical family, is an acceptable substitute.

PORTUGUESE CABBAGE SOUP WITH OLIVE OIL

SERVES 4–6

4–6 medium potatoes (1 per person)
1 onion, finely chopped
1lb dark green cabbage leaves (spring
    greens) or curly kale or cavalo nero
2 tablespoons extra virgin olive oil
Salt and ground black pepper

TO SERVE

Extra virgin olive oil
Salsa piri-piri

1. Put 2 quarts water into a roomy saucepan with the potatoes and onion. Bring to a boil, add salt, and cook for 20 minutes, or until the potatoes are perfectly tender.

2. Meanwhile, shred the cabbage very finely with a sharp knife: first cut out the hard white stalk and central vein of the cabbage leaves, then roll the leaves up in little bundles and shred finely right across the grain.

3. Mash the potato into the broth to thicken. Season with pepper and check for salt, then stir in the oil. Bring the broth back to a boil, then sprinkle in the shredded cabbage, stirring continuously, so that it feels the heat immediately. Bubble up fiercely for 3–4 minutes—just long enough to soften the leaves. The cabbage should retain a little bite and the soup remain as green as grass.

4. Ladle into soup bowls. Hand round a jug of extra virgin olive oil and salsa piri-piri for a touch of fieriness.

MIXED VEGETABLE SOUP

SERVES 4–6

2–3 fresh shallots or young leeks, thinly sliced

2–3 young carrots, chopped

1–2 ribs celery with their green, chopped

1 green pepper, seeded and diced

1lb small new potatoes, scrubbed, and halved

2 tablespoons extra virgin olive oil

1/2lb baby fava beans in their pods, diced

1/2lb freshly podded peas

2 tablespoons chopped fresh parsley

1 tablespoon wine vinegar

Salt and ground black pepper

Fresh bread, to serve

FOR THE SALSA ROMESCO

2 dried red bell peppers, seeded and soaked to swell

2 large ripe tomatoes

2 garlic cloves, crushed

1 teaspoon salt

2 tablespoons fresh white breadcrumbs, fried until crisp in a little olive oil

2 tablespoons toasted almonds

1 dried red chile, seeded and crumbled

2 tablespoons red wine vinegar

About 1 1/4 cups olive oil

1. Put the sliced shallots or leeks, carrots, celery, green pepper, and potatoes in a large saucepan with 1 quart water. Add 1 teaspoon salt and a turn of the pepper mill. Bring to a boil and stir in the olive oil. Reduce the heat to a simmer, cover loosely, and leave to cook for about 20 minutes, or until the potatoes are tender and the oil has blended into the broth.

2. Stir in the fava beans and peas, bubble up again and cook for another 5 minutes, adding more boiling water if necessary. The consistency should be midway between a stew and a soup. Stir in the chopped parsley and sharpen the broth with a little vinegar. Taste and adjust the seasoning.

3. To make the Salsa Romesco, roast the dried peppers and the tomatoes under a hot broiler until they blister and take color. Pop them into a plastic bag and leave to cool. Scrape the pulp from the skin of the peppers and skin the tomatoes, scooping out and discarding the seeds. Put both into a food processor. Add the garlic, salt, breadcrumbs, almonds, and dried red chile, and pulverize to a paste. Pour in the red wine vinegar and oil, and continue to process until the sauce is thick and shiny.

4. Serve in deep bowls, handing round the salsa romesco separately for people to stir into their soups. Accompany with plenty of good fresh bread, roughly chunked.

SHARP-AND-SOUR LETTUCE SOUP

A creamy, vinegar-sharpened, summer soup popular among the Saxon community, which established itself around Sibiu in Romania in medieval times.

SERVES 4–6

¼ stick (2 tablespoons) unsalted butter
2 crisp lettuces (iceberg or romaine), rinsed and shredded
¼ cup all-purpose flour
⅔ cup whole milk
2 large eggs
1 tablespoon white wine vinegar
2 tablespoons each chopped fresh dill and savory, to garnish

1. Melt the butter in a medium saucepan. Add the shredded lettuces and toss over the heat for 2–3 minutes, or until the leaves wilt. Add 3 cups water and bring to a boil. Turn down the heat and leave to simmer for about 20 minutes.

2. Meanwhile, mix the flour with 2 tablespoons milk until smooth. Whisk in the remainder of the milk, the eggs, and the vinegar. Whisk in a ladleful of the hot lettuce broth, then return everything to the pan and simmer gently until thick and creamy.

3. Ladle into warm bowls and sprinkle with chopped dill and savory.

TIP
As a tasty, non-vegetarian option, before adding the lettuce to the butter, sauté a diced bacon slice in the butter until the fat runs and the meat browns a little.

PEANUT SOUP WITH GREENS

A recipe popular in Ghana, where the choice of unusual greens includes several members of the Malva family, as well as the young leaves of sweet potato, squashes, and yam. African cooks like to present clean flavors in simple combinations.

SERVES 4–6

¾lb spinach or any other edible
  greens
1lb tomatoes, skinned, peeled, and
  chopped
6–8 spring onions, finely chopped
¾ cup unsalted, shelled, roasted
  peanuts
Salt and ground black pepper
1 teaspoon chile flakes, to garnish

1. Cook the spinach in a tightly lidded saucepan in the water that clings to the leaves after washing, sprinkling with ½ teaspoon salt to encourage the juices to run.

2. As soon as the leaves collapse and soften, remove the lid and add 1 quart water, the tomatoes, and chopped spring onions. Turn down the heat, cover loosely, and simmer for about 15 minutes, or until the tomato flesh has collapsed in the steam.

3. Meanwhile, crush all but a tablespoon of the peanuts in a food processor or blender.

4. Stir the crushed peanuts into the soup, cover loosely and simmer for 15 minutes more. Taste and adjust the seasoning.

5. Ladle into bowls and garnish with the reserved peanuts and a sprinkle of chile flakes.

GERMAN PUMPKIN SOUP

This is a delicate, transparent, amber-colored soup flavored with cinnamon, sharpened with vinegar, and enriched with butter.

SERVES 4–6

2¼lbs pumpkin flesh, chunked
1 short cinnamon stick
6 cloves
2 tablespoons white wine vinegar
½ stick (4 tablespoons) unsalted butter, cut into small pieces
About 1 teaspoon sugar
Salt and ground black pepper
TO SERVE
Pickled cucumbers
Rye bread

1. Put the pumpkin chunks into a saucepan with the cinnamon and cloves (stick the cloves in a piece of pumpkin for easy retrieval).

2. Add 2 cups water, bring to a boil, and reduce the heat. Cover the pan loosely and leave to cook gently for 20–30 minutes, or until the pumpkin is perfectly soft. Remove the spices and transfer the pumpkin with its cooking water to a food processor. Process until smooth—add a little more water if necessary.

3. Return the soup to the pan. Stir in the vinegar and reheat until boiling. Stir in the butter and season with salt, plenty of freshly ground black pepper and a little sugar to bring out the sweetness. Serve with pickled cucumbers and rye bread.

TIP
Don't be tempted to add cream or you'll lose the beautiful clarity of color and simplicity of flavor.

GREEN PEA SOUP WITH DUMPLINGS

This is the Danish version of an old favorite, made with dried peas in winter and fresh in summer. If shelling your own fresh peas, save the empty pods and cook them in enough water to cover for 20 minutes—liquidize, sieve, and use as the basis for the broth.

SERVES 4–6

1lb shelled peas (fresh or frozen)
3–4 spring onions or shallots, chopped
$2/3$ cup heavy cream
Salt and ground black pepper
White bread croûtons browned in butter, to serve

1. Put the peas and chopped spring onions or shallots in a medium saucepan with 2 cups water. Bring to a boil and reduce the heat. Leave to cook gently for 20–25 minutes, or until the peas are perfectly soft.

2. Push the contents of the pan through a sieve or purée in a food processor. Return the purée to the pan with half the cream (reserve the rest). Season with salt and pepper, and bring to a boil, stirring, to blend and avoid sticking.

3. Ladle into bowls and garnish each serving with a swirl of the reserved cream. Serve croûtons separately for people to add their own.

CROÛTONS
Heat $1/4$ stick (2 tablespoons) butter in a small saucepan until a faint blue haze rises. Sprinkle in 1 cup diced stale bread, and toss until crisp and golden. Transfer to paper towels to drain.

CAULIFLOWER & CUMIN SOUP

Cumin, one of those warm, earthy fragrances you would expect to find in a Moroccan souk, adds sophistication and a touch of the exotic to a creamy, cauliflower soup. It's a perfect marriage of opposites.

SERVES 4–6

1 small cauliflower, trimmed and separated into florets
1/2 stick (4 tablespoons) unsalted butter
2 medium onions, diced
1 teaspoon ground cumin
2 1/2 cups whole milk
Salt and ground black pepper
TO GARNISH
2–3 tablespoons diced tomato
1/2 teaspoon cumin seeds
2–3 cilantro sprigs

1. Cook the cauliflower florets for 15–20 minutes, in just enough lightly salted water to cover, until they become soft. Drain, reserving 1 1/4 cups of the cooking water.

2. Meanwhile, melt the butter in a medium saucepan and gently fry the onions until they soften—don't let them brown. Sprinkle with the cumin and remove from the heat.

3. Put the contents of the pan into a blender with the cauliflower and the reserved cooking water. Add the milk and process thoroughly until smooth.

4. Reheat until boiling and ladle into bowls. Garnish each portion with a teaspoon of diced tomato, a sprinkle of cumin seeds, and cilantro leaves.

ZUCCHINI & TOMATO SOUP

Make this in late summer and early fall with overgrown zucchini and the last of the summer's over-ripe, odd-sized tomatoes. It can be served hot or cold, as you please.

SERVES 4–6

2 tablespoons olive oil

1lb onions or shallots, skinned and chopped

1–2 ribs celery, thinly sliced

2¼lbs tomatoes, peeled and roughly chopped

1¼ cups vegetable or chicken stock (see page 16), if preferred

1lb zucchini

Salt

Grated Parmesan cheese, to serve

TO GARNISH

6 zucchini flowers, shredded, or the leaves from 3–4 basil sprigs

Balsamic vinegar

1. Heat the oil in a saucepan and fry the onions or shallots and celery gently until they lose their crispness. Add the tomatoes and bubble up, mashing with a fork to collapse the tomato to a thick purée. Add the stock, bring to a boil, cover and reduce the heat. Simmer for 15–20 minutes, then mash thoroughly or put everything into a food processor and process until smooth. Gently reheat.

2. Meanwhile, grate the zucchini into a colander, salt them lightly, and leave to drain for 10 minutes or so. Rinse to remove the excess salt.

3. Reheat the tomato and stock and stir in the grated zucchini. Bring back to a boil, reduce the heat, and simmer for 10 minutes more, or until the vegetables are soft and soupy.

4. Ladle into bowls, then finish with shredded zucchini flowers or basil leaves and a drop of balsamic vinegar. Hand round a bowl of grated Parmesan separately.

RUSSIAN BORSCHT

SERVES 4–6

1lb uncooked small beets
   with their leaves
4 tablespoons lard oil
1 onion, finely chopped
1 garlic clove, chopped
1 large carrot, diced
1 large parsnip, diced
1 small turnip, diced (include the
   leaves, if available)
1 quart vegetable or chicken stock
   (see page 16), if preferred
1 bay leaf
2 medium potatoes, peeled and diced
½lb boiling sausage, optional
About 1 teaspoon sugar
1 tablespoon vinegar
Salt and ground black pepper
⅔ cup sour cream, to serve

1. Rinse the beet and trim the leaves, leaving a generous tuft of stalk. Put one of the beets into a small pan with enough water to cover, bring to a boil, and cook gently for 20–30 minutes, or until perfectly tender. Set aside. Meanwhile, peel and grate the remaining beetroots, shred the leaves, and chop the stalks.

2. Put the lard or oil in a large saucepan. Add the onion and garlic, then fry until they take a little color. Stir in the grated raw beets, the carrot, parsnip, and turnip and turn them over in the heat for 1–2 minutes. Add the stock and bay leaf and bring to a boil. Reduce the heat and simmer gently for 10 minutes.

3. Add the diced potatoes and the boiling sausage, if using. Bring back to a boil and simmer for 12–15 minutes, or until the potatoes are soft. Stir in the shredded beet leaves and diced stalks. Bring back to a boil. Season with salt, pepper, a little sugar, and the vinegar. Simmer for 5–10 minutes more or until everything is soft.

4. Remove and slice the sausage, if using, and place a slice in each serving bowl. Skin and dice the reserved cooked beets, stir it into the broth, and watch the soup take on a beautiful crimson blush.

5. Ladle the soup into serving bowls and hand round a bowl of sour cream separately.

CHILLED RED PEPPER SOUP

SERVES 4–6

1 large onion, thinly sliced
2 tablespoons olive oil
3–4 ripe red bell peppers (about 1lb)
3 cups vegetable stock (see page 16) or beef or chicken stock (see pages 15 and 16), if preferred
About 1 tablespoon sherry or white wine vinegar
1/2 teaspoon hot pimentón (Spanish paprika) or chile powder
About 1 teaspoon sugar
Salt

TO GARNISH
Fresh marjoram leaves
Sesame seeds
Freshly ground black pepper

TO SERVE
Toasted country bread
Salt-cured anchovies
Olive oil

1. Fry the onion gently in the oil in a heavy saucepan until soft and golden—don't let it brown. This will take at least 15 minutes.

2. Meanwhile, roast the peppers by holding them on the end of a knife in a flame, turning them until the skin blackens and blisters. Alternatively, roast them in a very hot oven (450°F) or under the broiler, turning them frequently. Pop the hot peppers in a plastic bag, seal, and leave for 10 minutes to let the steam loosen the skins.

3. Cut the peppers in half, remove the seeds, and carefully scrape the flesh from the skins in long strips.

4. Save a few pepper strips for garnish and add the remaining pepper flesh to the onion in the pan. Add the stock, bubble up and cook for 10 minutes to marry the flavors.

5. Transfer the contents of the pan to a food processor. Add the sherry or vinegar and pimentón or chile, and process until smooth. Season with the sugar and a little salt. Leave to cool before transferring to the refrigerator to chill.

6. Check the seasoning before serving—you might need a little more vinegar, salt, or sugar. Garnish with the reserved pepper strips, a few marjoram leaves, and a sprinkle of sesame seeds and freshly ground black pepper. Serve with toasted country bread topped with salt-cured anchovies and a little olive oil.

POTATO SOUP WITH PINE NUTS

This Chilean potato soup is finished with toasted pine nuts. Potatoes are native to Chile's uplands and pine nuts, a crop gathered in the vast forests of the southern Andes, were an important protein source for the indigenous inhabitants of the region.

SERVES 4–6

2¼lbs old potatoes, thickly sliced
2½ quarts vegetable stock (see page 16) or beef stock (see page 15), or water, if preferred
1 large garlic clove, chopped
1 large onion, finely chopped
4 tablespoons pine nuts
Salt and ground black pepper
TO FINISH
1 tablespoon chopped fresh chives, to garnish

1. Put the potatoes in a large saucepan with the stock or water. Add the garlic and onion and bring to a boil. Reduce the heat, cover loosely, and cook for about 30 minutes, or until the potato has more or less collapsed into the broth. Mash roughly so that the soup stays fairly lumpy.

2. Meanwhile, lightly toast the pine nuts in a dry pan. Set aside 1 tablespoon for garnishing and crush the rest roughly. Stir the crushed pine nuts into the soup and simmer for a 10 minutes more.

3. Taste and adjust the seasoning. Ladle into bowls and garnish with the reserved pine nuts and chopped chives.

SPINACH & POMEGRANATE SOUP

This elegant rice and lentil soup, in the Persian tradition, is made with fresh spinach and garnished with pomegranate seeds.

SERVES 4–6

1lb spinach, stalks removed, rinsed
¼ stick (2 tablespoons) butter
1 large onion, finely chopped
1 tablespoon ground turmeric
2 tablespoons long-grain rice
2 tablespoons yellow split peas
½ teaspoon crushed black
   peppercorns
1 teaspoon salt
Juice and finely grated zest of 1 bitter
   orange or lemon
Seeds of 1 pomegranate, to garnish

1. Shred the spinach and set it aside.

2. Melt the butter in a large saucepan. Add the onion, turmeric, rice, split peas, peppercorns, and salt with enough fresh spring water to cover generously, about 1 quart. Bring to a boil, reduce the heat, and bubble gently for 20–30 minutes, or until the rice grains are tender and the split peas are perfectly soft. Stir in the spinach and bubble up again. Reduce the heat, and simmer for another 10 minutes, or until the spinach is well amalgamated into the soup. Stir in the citrus juice and zest, then taste and adjust the seasoning.

3. Ladle into bowls and garnish each portion with a sprinkle of pomegranate seeds.

TIP
Any leaf-vegetables can replace the spinach: chard, members of the cabbage family and any wild-gathered greens such as sorrel, dandelion, and mallow.

MONASTERY MUSHROOM SOUP WITH SOUR CREAM

SERVES 4–6

½lb mixed wild or cultivated
   mushrooms
2 tablespoons butter
1 tablespoon diced smoked
   bacon or ham (optional)
2 large leeks, thinly sliced
2–3 ribs celery, thinly sliced
1–2 large carrots, diced
1 bay leaf
1 thyme sprig
½ teaspoon freshly grated nutmeg
1 large potato, peeled and grated
Salt and ground black pepper
TO GARNISH
⅔ cup sour cream
2 tablespoons chopped fresh chives
   (or chopped leek green)
TO SERVE
Brown bread
Gouda or Edam cheese

1. Pick over the mushrooms, wipe the caps, trim the stalks, and slice. Melt the butter in a medium saucepan and stir in the mushrooms. Fry for a moment before adding the bacon or ham, if using. The wetter the fungi, the longer it takes to release their water and caramelize a little.

2. As soon as the mushrooms have yielded up their water and started to sizzle, add the leeks, celery, and carrots and fry for 5 minutes more, or until the vegetables soften. Add the herbs and $1\frac{1}{4}$ cups water and bring everything to a boil. Season with freshly grated nutmeg, salt, and pepper and reduce the heat. Cover loosely and leave to simmer for about 40 minutes.

3. Stir in the grated potato and bring back to a boil. Simmer for 10 minutes more, or until the potato is perfectly soft and has thickened the broth.

4. Check the seasoning and ladle into bowls. Garnish with a swirl of sour cream and a sprinkle of chopped chives. Serve with thick slabs of brown bread and Gouda or Edam cheese.

SPICY TOMATO SOUP

A fiery tomato soup from southern Italy, which gets its heat from peperoncini, the fierce little scarlet chile used to flavor and season instead of expensive imported peppercorns.

SERVES 4–6

2–3 tablespoons extra virgin olive oil
1 onion, finely chopped
2–3 garlic cloves, crushed
2–3 peperoncini or any fresh or
    dried chiles
2¼lbs tomatoes (fresh or canned),
    roughly chopped
1 thyme sprig
1 oregano sprig
Sugar, salt, and ground black pepper
TO GARNISH
2 tablespoons chopped fresh parsley
1 tablespoon black olives, pitted
    and chopped

1. Put all the ingredients except the seasonings into a large saucepan and leave to infuse for 30 minutes. Bring everything to a boil, then reduce the heat. Simmer gently over a low heat for 30 minutes. You shouldn't need to pay it much attention as the tomatoes produce plenty of liquid and there is little danger of sticking.

2. Push the tomato mixture through a fine-meshed sieve, leaving skin, seeds, and other debris behind.

3. Return the purée to the pan and dilute with water to the consistency that suits you (2 cups is a rough guide). Bring back to a boil and season with sugar, salt, and freshly ground black pepper.

4. Ladle into bowls and garnish with a sprinkling of chopped parsley and chopped pitted black olives.

LEEK SOUP

A satisfying winter-warmer from the Basque country, *purrusalda* ranks as the national dish of a region noted for a strong feeling of national identity. Packed with vitamins, it's honest, simple, and very good.

SERVES 4–6

6 large leeks, with their green tops
1 large potato, diced
⅓ cup olive oil
4 garlic cloves, halved vertically
Ground allspice or freshly grated
    nutmeg, to taste (optional)
2–3 tablespoons chopped fresh
    parsley
Salt and ground black pepper

1. Bring 1 quart water to a boil in a saucepan and salt lightly. Meanwhile, trim the leeks: discard the root and remove the tough outer leaves, but leave most of the green. Cut the leeks lengthways into long, thin ribbons. Stir the leeks into the boiling water, bubble up, and reduce the heat. Leave to simmer for 10 minutes, or until the leeks soften. Add the potato and bubble up again. Reduce the heat and cook gently for 15–20 minutes more, or until the potato is perfectly soft.

2. Meanwhile, warm the oil in a small frying pan and fry the garlic gently until small bubbles form around the edges and they start to brown. Remove the pan from the heat, take out the garlic and discard, reserving the oil.

3. Mash the potato into the broth just enough to thicken it a little. Stir in the garlicky oil and bubble up. Reduce the heat, then raise it again so that the oil and the broth form an emulsion.

4. Taste and season with salt and pepper and a little ground allspice or grated nutmeg, if liked. Stir in the parsley, then serve.

JERUSALEM ARTICHOKE SOUP WITH TAPENADE

The Jerusalem or root artichoke—no relation of the leafy globe artichoke—has a sweet, mild, aniseed flavor and, when cooked, a texture rather like turnip. In this recipe from Provençe, the soup's natural blandness is counter-pointed by the salty pungency of the tapenade.

SERVES 4–6

1lb Jerusalem artichokes
About 3 cups vegetable or chicken
   stock (see page 16), if preferred
1 teaspoon finely grated lemon zest
1 teaspoon ground asafoetida
Salt and ground black pepper
FOR THE TAPENADE
½ cup pitted black olives
1 garlic clove, chopped
2 tablespoons extra virgin olive oil
2–3 salt-cured anchovies
1 tablespoon pickled capers, chopped
2 tablespoons lemon juice

1. The knobbly shape of root artichokes makes them tricky to peel unless the skins are loosened first: boil them in a saucepan of salted water for 10 minutes, then rub off the papery covering. Cut the prepared roots into walnut-sized pieces, rinse, and transfer to a medium saucepan with the stock. Bring to a boil, turn down the heat, cover, and leave to cook until tender, about 25–30 minutes.

2. Put the artichokes and their cooking water into a food processor and process until smooth. Add the lemon zest and process again. Season with the asafoetida, pepper, and a little salt, then return the soup to the pan. Reheat gently, stirring to avoid sticking.

3. Meanwhile, make the tapenade. Mash the olives with the garlic, oil, anchovies, capers, and lemon juice, either in the processor or with a mortar and pestle, until you have a smooth paste.

4. Ladle the pale, creamy soup into warm bowls and finish with a swirl of the salty black tapenade—the contrast of color, flavor, and texture is wonderfully dramatic.

SPINACH & FENNEL BOUILLABAISSE

This fresh-flavored, spring soup takes its name from the cooking process, a matter of raising and dropping the temperature of the soup so the oil forms an emulsion with the broth. The *bouilla*, or boil-up, is quickly followed by the *abaisse*, or cool-down, with the process repeated several times in quick succession.

SERVES 4–6

2¼lbs spinach, stalks removed, shredded
1 large onion, finely chopped
1 fennel bulb, diced
1lb potatoes (yellow, for preference)
3 cups vegetable stock (see page 16) or water and 1 glass white wine
2 garlic cloves, finely chopped
2 tablespoons chopped fresh parsley
About 4 tablespoons olive oil
Salt and ground black pepper
4–6 poached eggs or shelled soft-boiled eggs (optional), to serve

1. Rinse the shredded spinach and set it aside.

2. Put the onion, fennel, and potatoes in a medium saucepan. Add the stock or water and wine. Season lightly. Bring everything to a boil, then reduce the heat. Simmer for 20 minutes, or until the potato is soft.

3. Stir in the spinach, garlic, and parsley, then return to a boil. Cook for 5–8 minutes more, or until the spinach has collapsed into the broth.

4. Stir the oil into the broth and bubble up. Reduce the heat until the soup is no longer bubbling, then bubble up again. Repeat at least twice, until you can no longer see traces of oil on the surface and the broth is slightly thickened. Serve in deep soup plates, with or without a poached or soft-boiled egg floated on each portion, if liked.

GAZPACHO

Andalusians often keep a pitcher of this in the refrigerator in summer, serving it well diluted with very cold water. To serve as a first-course soup, choose at least three of the optional extras for people to add their own.

SERVES 4–6

1 slice of day-old bread
2 tablespoons white wine vinegar
2 garlic cloves, crushed
2 tablespoons olive oil
1 small or ½ large cucumber, peeled
    and roughly chopped
2¼lbs tomatoes, peeled, seeded,
    and chopped
1 green bell pepper, seeded and diced
About 2 cups iced water
Salt and sugar

FOR THE ACCOMPANIMENTS

Hot croûtons (diced bread fried in
    a little olive oil)
Chopped hard-boiled egg
Diced serrano ham
Diced cucumber
Diced peppers
Tomato, skinned and diced
Mild onion, chopped

1. Tear the bread into small pieces. Put the bread pieces into a bowl containing 2 tablespoons water, the vinegar, and the garlics, and leave to soak for 10 minutes.

2. Transfer the bread and its soaking liquid to a blender or food processor. Add all the remaining ingredients except for the seasoning and process everything until smooth.

3. Add 1 cup water until you have the consistency you like, thick or thin, depending on whether you wish to serve your gazpacho as a refreshment or a soup. Adjust the seasoning with salt and a little sugar.

4. Transfer the gazpacho to a pitcher and cover securely. Set in a cold larder or the refrigerator for 2–3 hours, or until well chilled.

5. As a refreshment, serve the gazpacho in long, chilled glasses. As a first-course soup, ladle into bowls and hand round the extras separately for people to add their own.

TIP
The color of gazpacho is dependent on the ripeness of your tomatoes. For a warmer pink color choose very ripe tomatoes.

MINESTRONE

This thick soup, fortified with pasta and enriched with olive oil, is the classic midday meal of the farmers of northern Italy in winter. The vegetables are as variable as you please—just include whatever is local and in season.

SERVES 4

4 tablespoons olive oil

1 large onion, diced

2 large carrots, diced

2–3 ribs green celery (including the leaves), chopped

1¼ cups vegetable stock (see page 16) or ham stock (see pages 15), if preferred

1lb old potatoes, diced

1lb yellow or white turnips, peeled and diced

4 tablespoons short macaroni or any medium-sized pasta shapes

1lb shredded cabbage (cavalo nero or Savoy)

Salt and ground black pepper

2 tablespoons finely chopped fresh parsley

1 teaspoon finely grated lemon zest

1 garlic clove, finely chopped

TO SERVE

Olive oil, for drizzling

Parmesan cheese, for grating

1. Heat the oil in a large saucepan and fry the onion, carrot, and celery gently for about 10 minutes, or until the vegetables soften and take a little color (sprinkle them with a little salt to help the frying process). Add the stock, the diced potatoes and turnips, and bring everything to a boil. Allow one big bubble, turn down the heat, cover loosely, and simmer for about 15 minutes, or until the vegetables are nearly soft. Mash the vegetables a little to thicken the broth.

2. Stir in the macaroni or your chosen pasta, reboil, and cook for 10 minutes more. Stir in the shredded cabbage. Bring everything back to a boil and cook for 5 minutes more, or until both the pasta and cabbage are tender. The total cooking time will be about 30 minutes.

3. Just before you serve, stir in the chopped parsley, lemon zest, and garlic. Taste and adjust the seasoning. Ladle into warm soup bowls and serve with oil for drizzling and a chunk of Parmesan cheese and a grater.

CATALAN VEGETABLE SOUP

SERVES 4–6

4 tablespoons olive oil

1 large Spanish onion, thinly sliced

1 tablespoon diced serrano ham or lean bacon (optional)

2 red bell peppers, seeded and sliced

500g tomatoes, skinned, peeled, and diced (or use tinned)

1½ cups white wine

1lb pumpkin or winter squash, peeled, seeded, and diced

Salt and ground black pepper

FOR THE PICADA

2 garlic cloves, chopped

1 tablespoon toasted almonds

2 tablespoons chopped Italian parsley

1 teaspoon ground cinnamon

2–3 cloves

½ teaspoon ground cloves

6–8 saffron threads, soaked in 1 tablespoon boiling water

4–6 thick slices of sourdough bread

1–2 tablespoons olive oil

4–6 tablespoons grated cheese

1. Heat the oil in a saucepan and fry the onion and ham gently for 20 minutes, or until soft and golden. Remove and reserve. Drop in the pepper rings and fry them until they soften. Return the onions to the pan, add the diced tomatoes and the wine, and bubble fiercely until the tomato flesh collapses and the steam no longer smells of alcohol.

2. Add the pumpkin and pour in about 3 cups boiling water. Return to a boil, reduce the heat, and simmer for 20 minutes, or until the pumpkin is soft.

3. Meanwhile, blend the picada ingredients in a processor or pound in a mortar and pestle until you have a thick paste—you may need a little more water. Stir the picada into the soup and cook for 5 minutes, to blend the flavors.

4. Toast the bread on both sides and trickle each slice with a little olive oil. Top the toasts with grated cheese.

5. To serve, ladle the soup into heat-proof soup bowls and top each portion with its slice of bread and cheese. Slip the bowls under a hot broiler to melt the cheese.

VICHYSSOISE

A leek and potato soup, as they like it in France. You can serve it hot or cold, although the chilled version is the classic version. The only rule is that the volume of leek should equal that of the potato.

SERVES 4–6

2 large leeks, white part only, thinly
   sliced
2 large potatoes, chunked
Bouquet garni (bay leaf, thyme, and
   parsley, tied in a bunch)
²/₃ cup light cream
Salt and ground black pepper
Chopped chives, to garnish

1. Put the vegetables in a large saucepan with just enough water to cover —about 4 cups. Add the bouquet garni and a little salt. Bring to a boil and simmer for 30–40 minutes, or until the potatoes are perfectly soft.

2. Remove the bouquet garni. Put everything in a food processor and process until smooth. (For a thinner, more delicate purée, push the vegetables through a sieve.)

3. Add the cream and process until well blended. Taste and season generously with salt and pepper.

4. Leave to cool and transfer to the refrigerator to chill. Serve in bowls and garnish with a sprinkling of chives.

CHILLED TARRAGON SOUP

A recipe from Serbia, simple and easy to make, which can also be served hot in winter. The dill can be replaced with thyme, tarragon, or chervil, but keep it to a single herb. This way you can best appreciate an individual fragrance.

SERVES 4–6

1 large handful of fresh tarragon leaves (at least ¼ cup, plus stalks)
1 tablespoon finely chopped onion
1 tablespoon unsalted butter
1 tablespoon all-purpose flour
3 cups vegetable or chicken stock (see page 16), if preferred
1 cup white wine
2 egg yolks
½ cup sour cream
½ cup fresh spinach leaves, shredded
Salt and ground black pepper
Tarragon sprigs, to garnish

1. De-stalk the tarragon, shred the leaves finely, and reserve. Tie the stalks in a little bunch.

2. Fry the onion gently in the butter in a saucepan. As soon as the onion softens, stir in the flour and fry for another 2–3 minutes—don't let anything brown. Without removing the pan from the heat, gradually whisk in the stock, beating to avoid lumps. As soon as it boils, add the wine, bubble up, reduce the heat, and cook until the alcohol has evaporated and the steam no longer smells of wine.

3. Add the bunch of tarragon stalks, reduce the heat, and simmer gently for 10 minutes to cook the flour and marry the flavors.

4. Meanwhile, whisk the egg yolks with the sour cream until well blended, then whisk in a ladleful of the hot soup. Remove the pan from the heat, discard the tarragon stalks, then whisk in the egg and cream mixture, blending until smooth. Stir in the shredded tarragon and spinach leaves. Taste and adjust the seasoning. Leave to cool before transferring to the refrigerator to chill.

5. Ladle into soup bowls and garnish each serving with a sprig of tarragon.

CHILLED AVOCADO SOUP

The soft, buttery flesh of the avocado, the fruit of a Central American native tree, provides both thickening and flavor to this pretty Mexican soup.

SERVES 4–6

2 ripe avocados
$\frac{1}{2}$ cucumber, peeled and diced
1 green bell pepper, cored and seeded
$\frac{1}{2}$ mild onion, chopped
1 garlic clove, chopped
1 green chile, seeded and sliced
Juice of 2 limes (or lemons)
1 teaspoon salt
1 small bunch of fresh cilantro

TO SERVE

Quartered limes
Coarse sea salt
Tortilla chips (optional)

1. Halve, stone, and peel the avocados. Drop the flesh of the avocados into a food processor with the cucumber, green pepper, onion, garlic, chile, and lime juice. Add $1\frac{1}{4}$ cups ice-cold water and the salt. Process thoroughly until smooth.

2. Add a handful of fresh cilantro leaves and another $1\frac{1}{4}$ cups cold water. Process briefly—just long enough to chop the cilantro, which should still be visible as little flecks. Taste and adjust the seasoning, remembering that you will be handing round more salt with the lime quarters for people to add their own.

3. Serve chilled with lime quarters, coarse sea salt, and tortilla chips separately, if liked.

TIP
To serve hot, dilute with boiling chicken stock instead of cold water.

CHILLED CELERY SOUP WITH LEMON GREMOLATA

This is a fresh-flavored, summer soup that is quickly prepared and finished with the classic Italian flavoring mix. It can be served hot equally well.

SERVES 4–6

1 small head celery (green unblanched for preference)
1 tablespoon olive oil
1 onion, diced small
1 large potato, peeled and diced
1 bay leaf
Salt and ground black pepper
1¼ cups whole milk
Focaccia, to serve

FOR THE GREMOLATA

1 tablespoon parsley leaves
1 garlic clove, crushed
1 tablespoon finely grated lemon zest

1. Rinse and chop the celery ribs, reserving the heart.

2. Heat the olive oil in a medium saucepan and add the chopped onion. Fry gently until it softens—don't let it take color. Add the diced potato and the chopped celery ribs and continue to fry gently, loosely lidded, for 5 minutes. Add 3 cups water and bring to the boil. Add the bay leaf and salt and pepper, turn down the heat, and simmer for 10–15 minutes, until the vegetables are perfectly tender.

3. Remove the bay leaf and process the soup with the milk until smooth. Taste and adjust the seasoning, then chill.

4. Meanwhile, prepare the gremolata: chop the reserved celery heart, parsley, garlic, and lemon zest together until well blended.

5. Ladle the soup into bowls and garnish each portion with gremolata. Serve with focaccia hot from the oven.

CHILLED WATERCRESS SOUP

A simple, elegant soup that is given a peppery kick from the masses of watercress used—gorgeously green and summery. Take it on a picnic, as it's perfect with smoked salmon sandwiches.

SERVES 4–6

1 large bunch (about ½lb) of watercress
1 large leek, including the green tops, thinly sliced
1 large potato, chunked
3 cups vegetable or chicken stock (see page 16), if preferred
1 cup light cream
1 tablespoon lemon juice
Salt and ground black pepper

1. Rinse the watercress and strip the leaves from the stalks, reserving both in separate piles.

2. Put the leek, potato, and watercress stalks in a medium saucepan with the vegetable or chicken stock and 1 teaspoon salt. Bring to a boil, turn down the heat, and simmer gently for about 30 minutes, until the potato is tender enough to collapse into the broth.

3. Transfer the contents of the pan to a food processor. Process until smooth, or push through a sieve. Leave to cool.

4. Add the cream (saving a spoonful for garnishing), the lemon juice, and all but a few of the watercress leaves. Process again until the soup is pale green and well flavored with watercress. Taste and add salt and freshly ground pepper. Chill in the refrigerator for 1–2 hours.

5. Garnish the soup with the reserved watercress leaves and an extra swirl of cream.

CHILLED SORREL SOUP

A classic spring soup in the French tradition—creamy and sharp. If you cannot find sorrel, watercress and a squeeze of lemon will fool all but the keenest palate.

SERVES 4

2 generous handfuls of sorrel leaves, rinsed and shredded
¼ stick (2 tablespoons) butter
3 cups strong vegetable or chicken stock (see page 16), if preferred
¼ cup all-purpose flour
½ cup heavy cream
Salt and ground black pepper

TO GARNISH
A little more heavy cream
A few sorrel leaves, shredded

TO SERVE
Crusty rolls
Unsalted butter

1. Drop the sorrel in a saucepan with a pinch of salt and the butter, cover tightly, and shake over the heat for 2–3 minutes, or until the leaves collapse.

2. Drop the contents of the pan into a blender or food processor with the chicken stock and the flour and process until smooth. Alternatively, finely chop the sorrel, blend with the flour, and add the stock.

3. Tip everything back into the pan and bring to a boil, whisking until it thickens a little and no longer tastes of raw flour. Whisk in the cream. Check the seasoning and add salt and pepper to taste. Remove the pan from the heat and leave to cool.

4. Serve chilled, with a swirl of cream and the shredded sorrel. Serve with hot crusty rolls and unsalted butter.

TIP
To gather your own sorrel from the wild, look out for the pointed, heart-shaped dark green leaves: check in the manual first time round, although the shape as well as the sharp, lemony flavor is unmistakable.

CHILLED ASPARAGUS SOUP

The grassy flavor of the asparagus comes through clear and true in this pretty, green soup. Perfect for the first days of summer, followed by a plate of cold ham or chicken with a new potato salad.

SERVES 4–6

1lb green asparagus, trimmed
½lb potatoes, diced
3–4 spring onions, diced
1 bay leaf
2½ cups vegetable or chicken stock (see page 16), if preferred
1¼ cups light cream
Salt and ground black pepper
⅔ cups sour cream, to garnish

1. Chop the asparagus into short lengths, reserving the tips.

2. Put the asparagus, potatoes, spring onions, and bay leaf into a large saucepan with the stock. Bring to a boil, cover, and reduce the heat. Cook for 20 minutes, or until the potatoes are soft.

3. Push everything through a sieve to remove the stringy stalks. Transfer to a food processor with the cream and process until smooth. Season with salt and pepper. Leave to cool, then transfer to the refrigerator to chill.

4. When you are ready to serve, drop the asparagus tips in boiling salted water for 2–3 minutes—just long enough to take the edge off their crispness. Remove with a slotted spoon and pass them under the cold faucet to keep them fresh and green.

5. Ladle the soup into bowls and garnish each serving with a swirl of sour cream and a few asparagus tips.

CHILLED TOMATO CREAM WITH FRESH BASIL

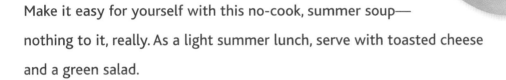

Make it easy for yourself with this no-cook, summer soup—

nothing to it, really. As a light summer lunch, serve with toasted cheese

and a green salad.

SERVES 4–6

2½ cups tomato juice
1¼ cups light cream
1 teaspoon sugar
2–3 drops Tabasco or chile sauce
TO GARNISH
3–4 basil sprigs, leaves only
1 tablespoon grated lemon zest

1. Combine the tomato juice with the cream in a food processor.

2. Add the sugar and a few drops of Tabasco or chile sauce, then chill in the refrigerator for a couple of hours.

3. Ladle into soup bowls. Garnish with basil leaves and grated lemon zest.

CHILLED YOGURT SOUP WITH CUCUMBER, WALNUTS, & DILL

A fresh yogurt soup stirred with grated cucumber, crushed walnuts, and dill, just as they like it in Turkey. For a taste from a taverna along the Bosphorus, serve with mussel fritters and a garlicky eggplant dip.

SERVES 4–6

1 small or ½ large cucumber, grated
3 cups natural yogurt
2 tablespoons shelled walnuts
2–3 garlic cloves, grated
1 small bunch of dill, leaves only
Salt

1. Grate the cucumber and sprinkle with salt. Leave to drain in a colander for half an hour.

2. Whisk the yogurt with 4 tablespoons cold water until well blended.

3. Wrap the walnuts in a clean cloth, and crush them with a rolling pin.

4. Rinse the cucumber and stir into the yogurt with the crushed walnuts, garlic, and dill (keeping some aside as garnish).

5. Transfer to the refrigerator until you are ready to serve.

6. Ladle the soup in soup bowls and sprinkle with the remaining dill, roughly chopped.

PULSES &
GRAINS

PROVENÇAL BEAN SOUP WITH PISTOU

A creamy, lima bean soup finished with the Provençal version of pesto genovese —olive oil, basil, and garlic. Traditionally it's vegetarian fasting food for Lent, so meat is not included and the pistou provides the flavoring.

SERVES 4–6

1¼ cups butter beans, soaked
   overnight
2 quarts unsalted vegetable stock
   (see page 16) or water
1 bay leaf
½ teaspoon crushed black
   peppercorns
1 large potato, peeled and diced
Sea salt
TO SERVE
Grated cheese (Cantal or Parmesan)
Rustic white bread
FOR THE PISTOU
4–6 fresh, plump garlic cloves
   (1 for each person)
¼ cup basil leaves, stripped from
   their stems
1 slice of day-old bread
⅔ cup extra virgin olive oil

1. Drain the beans and put them in a saucepan with the stock or water, the bay leaf, and crushed peppercorns—no salt. Bring to a boil, skim off the gray foam that rises and reduce the heat to a simmer. Cover and leave to cook gently for 1 hour. Add the potato and continue to cook for a 30 minutes more, or until the beans are soft. Check regularly and add more boiling water as needed.

2. Meanwhile, put all the pistou ingredients in a food processor or blender and process until smooth. Alternatively, pound the garlic, basil leaves, and bread with a pestle in a mortar, then add the oil gradually until you have a thick, "spoonable" emulsion.

3. When the beans and potatoes are soft, season with salt. Mash or process a ladleful and stir it back into the soup to thicken the broth.

4. Ladle into soup plates, finish each serving with a swirl of pistou, and hand round the remainder separately with a bowl of grated cheese and some fresh rustic bread.

NAVY BEAN SOUP WITH CABBAGE

This robust, lunchtime soup from Galicia, Spain's northwesterly province, *caldo gallego*, the national dish of the region, is a complete meal in itself. Serve with good bread for mopping.

SERVES 4–6

½lb navy, lima, or flageolet beans, soaked overnight
1lb salt pork or unsmoked bacon, diced
1lb tender young turnips, chopped
2¼lbs old potatoes, peeled and chopped
1 small Savoy cabbage or 1lb spring greens, finely shredded
1 tablespoon diced serrano ham
Salt and ground black pepper

TIP
Grelos (turnip-tops) the traditional greens of the Galicia region, have a powerful mustard flavor. If unobtainable, choose any of the dark-leaf, well-flavored cabbages—curly kale, spring greens, or cavalo nero.

1. Drain the beans and put them in a large saucepan with 2 quarts water. Bring to a boil, skim off the gray foam that rises, and add the pork or bacon. Reduce the heat to a gentle bubble. Cover loosely and leave to cook for 1–1½ hours, or until the beans are perfectly tender, adding more boiling water as necessary and making sure the level of water remains roughly constant. When the beans are soft, taste, and season with salt and pepper.

2. Ladle half the broth into another saucepan, bring to a boil, and add the diced turnips. Return to a boil and add the potatoes. Simmer for 15 minutes, or until the vegetables are nearly soft.

3. Add the shredded leaves and the diced serrano ham. Bring back to the boil, cover, and cook for 6–10 minutes more, or until the cabbage is tender but still green.

4. Stir the contents of one pan into the other and serve the soup in deep soup bowls—or hand the two panfuls separately for people to combine as they please.

SPANISH GREEN LENTIL SOUP

SERVES 4–6

½lb lentils (the greeny-brown ones)

2 tablespoons olive oil

1 onion, chopped

4–5 garlic cloves, unskinned

1 tablespoon diced serrano ham

2 ribs celery, chopped

1 large tomato, peeled and chopped

1 dried red pepper, Ñora, seeded and
   torn or 1 tablespoon pimentón
   (Spanish paprika)

3–4 cloves

½ teaspoon black peppercorns,
   crushed

1 bay leaf

1 large potato, peeled and diced

Salt and ground black pepper

2 handfuls of spinach or chard leaves,
   shredded

2–3 tablespoons olive oil

1 tablespoon each of chopped fresh
   marjoram and parsley, to garnish

1. Put the lentils in a medium saucepan with 1½ quarts water and bring to a boil.

2. Heat the olive oil in a small frying pan and fry the onion, garlic, and ham until they sizzle and begin to brown.

3. Add the contents of the frying pan to the soup pan along with the remaining ingredients except the potato. Bring back to a boil and cover loosely.

4. Reduce the heat and leave to simmer for 40 minutes, or until the lentils are beginning to soften. Add the potato and bring everything back to a boil. Season, then turn down to a simmer. Cook for 15–20 minutes more, or until the potatoes and lentils are soft. (Lentils need about 1 hour's cooking in all, when they should be quite soft—if they're old, they'll take longer.) Top up with boiling water, if necessary.

5. To finish, stir in the shredded spinach or chard and bubble up for 5 minutes. Stir in the olive oil, taste, and adjust the seasoning. Serve garnished with marjoram or parsley.

ITALIAN BARLEY BROTH WITH WILD GREENS

A translucent barley broth, fortified with new potatoes, and sharpened with peppery wild greens, this soup is popular in Carnia, on Italy's border with Austria. In these border regions a wide variety of wild greens are gathered in spring, among them dandelion, chickweed, field poppy, and bladder campion.

SERVES 4–6

2 tablespoons olive oil
1 onion, diced
1 carrot, diced
1 rib celery, diced
1 quart vegetable stock (see page 16)
¼ cup pearl barley, soaked for 2 hours
1lb new potatoes, scrubbed and quartered
500g peppery greens (failing wild gatherings, use arugula, sorrel, frizzy endive, watercress, chervil, or spinach), rinsed and shredded
4–5 spring onions or wild garlic (leaves only), chopped
Juice and grated zest of 1 lemon
Salt and ground black pepper
Grated Parmesan cheese, to serve

1. In a medium saucepan, heat the oil and fry the onion, carrot, and celery until they soften a little. Add the stock, stir in the barley and its soaking water and bring everything to a boil. Turn down the heat and let it simmer for 40–45 minutes, or until the barley is tender and has thickened the broth.

2. Add the potatoes—the pieces should be about the size of a blackbird's egg—and bring back to a boil. Stir in the greens and the spring onions or wild garlic. Bring back to a boil and cook for 5 minutes more. Season with salt and pepper.

3. Stir in the lemon zest and enough juice to sharpen the flavor. (The wilder the greens, the less lemon you'll need.)

4. Ladle into soup bowls and hand round a bowl of grated Parmesan cheese separately.

YORKSHIRE MUSHY PEA SOUP

A thick, rib-sticking soup made with dried marrowfat peas, a storecupboard staple in the farmhouses tucked into the folds of the Yorkshire moors.

SERVES 4–6

½lb dried marrowfat peas, soaked overnight
1 quart ham or bacon or beef stock (see page 15)
1¼ cups milk
1 onion, diced
1 carrot, scraped and diced
2–3 ribs celery, diced
1 parsnip, diced
¼ stick (2 tablespoons) butter or lard
Salt and ground black pepper

TO GARNISH

2 tablespoons chopped fresh parsley
¼–½ stick (2–4 tablespoons) cold butter

1. Drain the peas and put them in a saucepan with the stock. Bring to a boil, reduce the heat, and leave to simmer until the peas are mushy—about 40–50 minutes. Stir in the milk.

2. Meanwhile, in a frying pan fry the vegetables gently in the butter or lard until they soften. Combine the contents of the two pans, stirring to blend. Taste and adjust the seasoning, then reheat well.

3. Ladle into bowls and garnish with a sprinkle of chopped parsley and a pat of butter.

TIP
For a vegetarian version, make the soup with a vegetable stock or plain water.

GREEK FAVA BEAN & FENNEL SOUP

A soup oozing with a combination of flavors popular on the islands of the Aegean, this fresh, summery soup is finished with egg and lemon, the classic thickening of the Greek kitchen.

SERVES 4–6

2¼lbs shelled fava beans
1 onion, chopped
1 fennel bulb, chopped
1 teaspoon grated lemon zest
Juice of ½ lemon
4 tablespoons olive oil
4 cups water
⅔ cup white wine
1 egg whisked with the juice of
   ½ lemon
Salt and ground black pepper
TO GARNISH
2 chopped spring onions
2 tablespoons chopped fennel fronds
   or dill
TO SERVE (OPTIONAL)
Quartered lemon
Fresh bread

1. Pick over the fava beans and slip them out of their skins.

2. Put the beans in a large saucepan with the remaining ingredients, except the egg, and bring everything to a boil. Cover and simmer for about 30 minutes, or until the beans are quite tender.

3. Remove the soup from the heat. Whisk a ladleful of the hot broth into the egg and lemon mixture, then whisk it back into the soup. Reheat gently without reboiling or the egg will scramble. Garnish with a sprinkle of chopped spring onions and fennel fronds or dill.

4. Serve with lemon quarters and plenty of bread to mop up the broth, if liked.

ITALIAN BEAN & MACARONI SOUP

SERVES 4–6

½ cup navy beans, soaked for 6 hours
  or overnight
1½ quarts ham or vegetable stock
  (see pages 15 and 16)
1 large carrot, diced
2–3 ribs celery, chopped
½ teaspoon crushed black
  peppercorns
2 bay leaves
1 teaspoon dried oregano
1 large tomato, peeled and diced,
  or about ½lb diced pumpkin
¼ cup macaroni or any medium-sized
  pasta shapes
1lb dark green leaves (such as
  cabbage, kale, turnip tops),
  shredded
Salt and ground black pepper

TO GARNISH
2 tablespoons fresh Italian parsley,
  chopped
Extra virgin olive oil

1. Drain the navy beans and put them in a large saucepan with the stock. Bring to a boil and skim off the gray foam that rises. Add the carrot, celery, peppercorns, bay leaves, and oregano. Bring back to a boil and reduce the heat a little. Bubble gently for 1 hour, or until the broth is well flavored and the beans are soft but not yet mushy.

2. Remove the bay leaves and stir in the diced tomato or pumpkin. Bring back to a boil. Add a little salt, stir in the pasta, and return to a boil. Bubble up for 15 minutes more, or until the pasta is nearly soft. Stir in the shredded leaves, bring back to the boil, and cook for 5 minutes more, or until everything is tender. Check and adjust the seasoning.

3. Ladle into bowls and garnish each bowl with chopped parsley and a swirl of olive oil. Hand round more olive oil for people to add as they please.

PERUVIAN QUINOA & PUMPKIN SOUP

A smooth, sweet soup flavored with hot yellow chile, Peru's super-fiery capsicum. The combination is very ancient: all three ingredients are native to the Andean plateau. Quinoa—pronounced keenwa—is remarkably high in protein and was the grain food of the Incas.

SERVES 4–6

½ cup quinoa
1lb pumpkin or winter squash
   flesh, diced
1 quart vegetable or chicken stock
   (see page 16)
½ stick (4 tablespoons) unsalted
   butter or olive oil
Juice and finely grated zest of 1 lime
Salt and ground black pepper
TO GARNISH
2 fresh yellow chiles, seeded and
   finely chopped
1 small bunch of basil, leaves torn
TO SERVE
Quartered limes
Unsalted tortilla chips

1. Rinse the quinoa under running water until the water runs clear. Transfer to a saucepan and cover with twice its own volume of water. Bring to a boil, reduce the heat, and cook gently until the grains are translucent and have popped, revealing little bands of white, about 20 minutes.

2. Meanwhile, put the pumpkin in a pan with the stock. Bring to the boil, reduce the heat, and cook until the pumpkin flesh is soft and mushy, about 15–20 minutes.

3. Transfer to a food processor, put in the butter or oil, and process until smooth.

4. Return the soup to the pan and reheat. Stir in the quinoa, lime juice and zest, then taste and adjust the seasoning.

5. Ladle into bowls and garnish with chopped chiles and a few torn basil leaves. Serve with quartered limes and tortilla chips.

BORLOTTI BEAN SOUP WITH SOUR CREAM

This fortifying soup, rich with sour cream and flavored with onion and bacon, is eaten at midday during the winter months in Holland. Something of a national treasure, the exact recipe is recorded in a popular folk song.

SERVES 4–6

1½ cups borlotti beans, soaked
   overnight
1 large potato, diced
6–8 slices bacon, diced
2–3 tablespoons fresh pork lard
   or butter
2 medium onions, peeled and diced
Salt and ground black pepper
1 cup sour cream, to garnish

1. Drain the beans and put them in a saucepan. Cover them generously with fresh water. Bring them to a boil, skim, and reduce the heat. Cook, loosely covered, until perfectly tender—allow 1–2 hours depending on the freshness of the beans. As soon as they are soft, add the potato, bring back to the boil, and season with salt and pepper. Cook until the potato is tender, about 15–20 minutes, adding more boiling water, if necessary.

2. Meanwhile, fry the bacon in its own fat until crisp and brown—you may need a little butter or lard. Remove and reserve.

3. Melt the remaining butter or lard in the pan drippings. Add the onions and fry until soft and golden, about 10 minutes. Return the bacon to the pan. Stir the onion, bacon, and the oily drippings into the soup.

4. Ladle into soup bowls and garnish each portion with a spoonful of sour cream.

MEXICAN BLACK BEAN SOUP

Black beans have a delicate, nutty flavor that is well served in this simple soup. The finishing enrichment, a buttery avocado mash, is added at the end in much the same way as an aioli is added to France's *pot au feu*.

SERVES 4–6

½lb dried black beans, soaked for no more than 6 hours or 2 x 14ozs cans ready-cooked black beans, drained
1 quart ham stock (see page 15)
Salt
FOR THE MASHED AVOCADO
1 large or 2 small ripe avocados
1 green chile, seeded and diced
Juice of 2 limes
2 tablespoons chopped fresh cilantro, plus extra to garnish
TO SERVE (OPTIONAL)
Quartered limes
Chilli flakes
Soft tortillas

1. Drain the beans of their soaking water and put them in a flameproof casserole. Add 1 quart boiling water—enough to cover the beans generously. Bring to simmering point, then turn down the heat. Cover tightly and leave to cook gently. Alternatively, cook them in the oven preheated to 325°F. Keep an eye on them and add hot water if necessary. Leave them to cook for as long as it takes for the skins to soften completely, about 2 hours (the fresher the beans, the quicker they will cook). Add salt after the beans soften completely.

2. Put the beans and their liquor into a food processor or blender and process to a purée. Dilute with boiling water to a spooning consistency.

3. If using canned beans, drain and process to a purée with the stock.

4. Meanwhile, mash the avocado flesh with the chopped chile, lime juice, and coriander.

5. Reheat the soup, then ladle into soup bowls. Top each portion with a spoonful of the spicy mashed avocado and an extra sprinkle of cilantro.

6. Serve with quartered limes, chile flakes, and soft tortillas, if liked.

CHICKPEA SOUP WITH CHEESE & EGG

A Sunday soup from Marseilles that is thickened with lemon and egg, Greek-style. Romantics serve it on the Sunday before Easter to commemorate the miraculous arrival of a Greek ship laden with chickpeas during a time of terrible famine.

SERVES 4–6

1¼ cups chickpeas, soaked overnight
1 large onion, finely chopped
2 carrots, diced
2 ribs celery, chopped
1 teaspoon grated lemon zest
1–2 sprigs each of rosemary
   and thyme
1–2 bay leaves
4 tablespoons olive oil
2 eggs beaten with the juice of
   1 lemon and 2 tablespoons
   of grated cheese
Salt and ground black pepper

TO SERVE

Fresh country-style bread
Grated cheese

1. Drain the soaked chickpeas. Bring 1½ quarts water to a boil in a large saucepan. Add the chickpeas and the remaining ingredients, except the salt and egg mixture. Bring back to a boil. Cover tightly and leave to cook at a rolling simmer for about 2 hours. Salt the soup when the chickpeas are soft.

2. Whisk a ladleful of the hot broth into the egg mixture, then whisk it back into the soup. Squish the chickpeas down a bit. Do not reboil or the eggs will curdle and your lovely velvety thickening will separate. Serve with bread, handing round more grated cheese separately.

CHESTNUT SOUP

This sophisticated soup, enriched with butter and egg yolks, makes good use of an ingredient that was one of the most important staple foodstuffs of the Mediterranean littoral until the New World staples, potatoes and maize, replaced the chestnut woods.

SERVES 4–6

1½ cups dried chestnuts, soaked
  overnight
1 quart chicken stock (see page 16)
  or water with 1 glass of white wine
1 tablespoon sugar
½ stick (4 tablespoons) butter
2 egg yolks, forked to blend
Salt and ground black pepper
TO GARNISH
1¼ cups thick strained sheep's milk
  yogurt (or any plain, thick yogurt)
1 tablespoon chopped fresh
  marjoram

1. Drain the chestnuts and bring them to a boil in a medium saucepan with the stock or water and wine, the sugar, and the butter. Reduce the heat to low, cover tightly, and simmer for 30–40 minutes, or until the chestnuts are soft.

2. Put everything into a food processor and process until smooth. Add the egg yolks to the mixture and process until well blended.

3. Return the soup to the pan and reheat gently—don't let it boil. Taste and add salt and freshly ground pepper.

4. Ladle into bowls and garnish each portion with a spoonful of yogurt and chopped marjoram.

TIP
*To prepare fresh chestnuts
for the pot, slit the skins and
roast them for half an hour in
a low oven. Peel them when
they're cool enough
to handle.*

SPICY CHICKPEA SOUP

A recipe from southern India, this vegetarian soup—flavored with asafoetida, sharpened with lemon juice, and spiked with chile—conforms to Hindu dietary rules.

SERVES 4—6

2½ cups cooked chickpeas (boiled without salt)
Juice of 2 lemons
2 tablespoons coarse salt
2 tablespoons mustard seed oil
2 teaspoons black mustard seeds
2–3 small dried red chiles, crumbled (or fresh chiles, seeded and diced)
1 tablespoon ground asafoetida
Chapatis or other flatbreads, to serve

TO GARNISH
2 tablespoons flaked coconut, lightly toasted
2 tablespoons chopped fresh cilantro

1. Put the chickpeas in a food processor or blender with 1 quart water, the lemon juice, and salt. Process until smooth. Transfer to a saucepan and heat, stirring regularly, until it boils.

2. Heat the oil gently in a frying pan, then add the mustard seeds—they jump like fleas when they feel the heat, so have a pan lid handy. Add the chiles and leave to sizzle for a few seconds. Add the asafoetida, then immediately stir the panful into the bean soup.

3. Ladle into soup bowls and garnish with flakes of toasted coconut and chopped cilantro. Serve with chapatis or other flatbreads.

TIP
Asafoetida, a dried resin prepared from the root of the giant fennel, is the substitute for onion and garlic in Hindu vegetarian cooking.

PORTUGUESE RED BEAN SOUP

This robust country soup, also known as *sopa de pedra* (stone soup), is traditional to the farming communities of Lisbon's hinterland.

SERVES 4–6, GENEROUSLY

1 cup red kidney, pinto, or borlotti
  beans, soaked overnight

¼lb pork belly skin, cut into
  thin slivers

1 chouriço negro, morcela, or similar
  black pudding or ¼lb soft chorizo

1 large onion, finely diced

6 garlic cloves, chopped

1 bay leaf

½ teaspoon white peppercorns

2 small turnips, diced

1 large carrot, diced

1lb waxy potatoes, peeled
  and diced

Salt and ground black pepper

1 generous handful of chopped fresh
  cilantro, to garnish

Salsa piri-piri sauce, to serve

1. Drain the beans and put them in a large saucepan with enough cold water to cover generously. Bring to a boil, drain, and return the beans to the pan. Add 2 quarts fresh water and bring back to a boil. Skim off any gray foam that rises.

2. Add the pork belly skin, with the sausage, onion, garlic, and bay leaf. Add the peppercorns. Bring to a boil, reduce the heat, and cover loosely. Keep the pan bubbling gently for as long as it takes to tenderize the beans, about 1–2 hours. If you need to add water, make sure it is boiling. Remove the sausage, slice neatly, and keep it warm. Taste and season the broth.

3. Add the turnips, carrot, and potatoes to the pan, and bubble up for 15–20 minutes more, or until the vegetables are tender. Add more boiling water if it looks like drying out, remembering that this soup should be very thick and dense with vegetables.

4. Add a generous handful of chopped cilantro, then ladle into bowls and hand round salsa piri-piri or some other hot sauce for people to add their own.

CHICKPEA & GINGER SOUP

SERVES 4–6

1 cup chickpeas, soaked overnight
2 quarts unsalted chicken or
    vegetable stock (see page 16)
¼ cup red lentils
1 onion, finely chopped
2 tablespoons tomato paste
1 short cinnamon stick
1 tablespoon ground ginger
1 teaspoon ground cumin
1 teaspoon ground turmeric
2–3 dried chiles, seeded and
    crumbled
Salt and ground black pepper
TO GARNISH
3–4 tablespoons olive oil
1 handful of fresh cilantro, chopped,
    leaves only
1 handful of fresh mint, chopped,
    leaves only
TO SERVE (OPTIONAL)
Quartered lemon
Pitta bread

1. Drain and rinse the chickpeas, then put them in a large saucepan with the stock. Bring to a boil and simmer for at least 2 hours, or until tender—don't add salt or allow the pan to come off the boil. Add more boiling water as necessary to maintain the volume.

2. When the chickpeas are perfectly soft, stir in the lentils, onion, tomato paste, and spices. Season with salt and pepper. Bring back to a boil and simmer for 30 minutes more, or until the lentils are mushy and the soup is satisfyingly thick.

3. Garnish with a swirl of olive oil and a generous handful of chopped cilantro and mint.

4. Serve in deep bowls, with lemon quarters for squeezing and soft pitta bread for mopping, if liked.

CARIBBEAN RED BEAN SOUP

A creamy, red bean soup with rice and finished with sazon, a seasoning paste used as a finishing ingredient among the islands. This is the version popular in the Dominican Republic.

SERVES 4–6

1 cup red beans (pinto, borlotti, or cranberry beans), soaked overnight
2–3 shallots, diced
$\frac{1}{3}$ cup long-grain rice

FOR THE SEASONING MIX
2 tablespoons olive oil or ¼ stick (2 tablespoons) butter
2 garlic cloves, finely chopped
1 medium onion, finely chopped
1 red pepper, seeded and finely chopped
2 tablespoons tomato paste

1. Drain the beans and put them in a saucepan with 2 quarts water. Bring to a boil and skim off the gray foam that rises. Stir in the shallots, reduce the heat, and cover loosely. Leave to bubble gently for 1 hour, or until the beans have softened but not yet collapsed.

2. Stir in the rice, adding more boiling water to make up the original volume, and cook for 20 minutes more, or until the rice is tender and the beans are almost mushy. Mash a little to thicken the broth.

3. Meanwhile, prepare the seasoning mix. Heat the oil or butter in a heavy frying pan and fry the garlic, onion, and pepper gently until soft— allow 10 minutes—without letting the mixture brown. Add the tomato paste, diluted with 2 tablespoons water, then bubble up, stirring to blend.

4. Ladle the soup into bowls and serve each portion with a spoonful of the seasoning mix.

SPICED GREEN LENTIL SOUP

This thick, nourishing lentil soup, flavored with cinnamon and cumin, is eaten in Lebanon at sunset during Ramadan.

SERVES 6

2 shallots or 4–5 spring onions, finely chopped
2–3 garlic cloves, finely chopped
3–4 tablespoons oil
1¼ cups green lentils
½ teaspoon ground cumin
½ teaspoon ground cinnamon
½ teaspoon crushed dried chiles
1 large potato, diced
Salt and ground black pepper

TO GARNISH
2 tablespoons chopped fresh cilantro
2–3 spring onions, finely chopped

1. In a large saucepan, fry the chopped onions and garlic gently in the oil until soft and golden—don't let them brown.

2. Add the lentils and stir over the heat. Pour in 2¼ quarts water and add the spices. Bring to a boil and season with salt and pepper. Reduce the heat and simmer for 10 minutes.

3. Add the diced potato, then bring back to a boil and cook gently for 30 minutes more, or until the lentils are soupy and the potato is perfectly soft.

4. Taste and adjust the seasoning. Garnish with a sprinkle of cilantro and finely chopped spring onions.

TIP
Serve with khobz, the Lebanese pitta bread that comes sprinkled with black nigella seeds, and fresh dates if they're in season.

MUNG BEAN SOUP WITH CASHEW NUTS

This spicy vegetarian soup, made with mung beans, is garnished with toasted cashews. Being meatless, it conforms to Hindu dietary rules.

SERVES 4–6

4 tablespoons ghee or ½ stick (4 tablespoons) unsalted butter
½ cup split mung beans, soaked for 6 hours
⅓ cup long-grain rice
1 teaspoon salt
1 teaspoon cumin seeds
1 teaspoon cracked black pepper
1 tablespoon chopped fresh ginger root
½ teaspoon crushed, dried chile
2 tablespoons toasted cashew nuts, roughly chopped, to garnish

1. Heat half the ghee or butter in a medium saucepan. Drain the beans and add to the pan. Fry, stirring, for 1–2 minutes. Add the rice and stir briefly over the heat until the grains turn transparent and are coated with fat.

2. Add 1½ quarts water with the salt and bring to a boil. Stir to break up the lumps and reduce the heat. Cover loosely and bubble up for 10 minutes. Stir again, cover tightly, and reduce the heat to a simmer. Leave to cook gently for 50 minutes more, or until the beans are mushy and the rice is tender.

3. Meanwhile, in a small frying pan, heat the remaining ghee or butter. Add the spices and let them sizzle for a few seconds. Stir the contents of the pan into the soup right at the end of the cooking.

4. Ladle into bowls and garnish with the toasted cashew nuts.

TIP
Serve with one of the soft, chewy Indian breads: chapati, paratha or naan.

FLAGEOLET & POLENTA SOUP WITH BLUE CHEESE

Flageolets, small green haricot beans, are popular in Cantabria in northern Spain. Here, a delicate bean soup is thickened with polenta, known in the region as Indian corn, a folk memory of its American origins. The finishing touch is Cabrales, a very strong blue cheese matured in maple leaves.

SERVES 4–6

1 cup flageolet beans, soaked
   overnight or 2 x 450g tins, drained
1½ quarts ham or vegetable stock
   (see pages 15 and 16)
1 bay leaf
A short length of ham bone
   (optional)
1 tablespoon diced serrano ham
2 tablespoons pork lard or ¼ stick
   (2 tablespoons) butter
1 tablespoon fine ground polenta
Salt and ground black pepper
¼lb crumbled Cabrales blue cheese
   (or other), to garnish

1. Drain the flageolet beans and put them in a medium saucepan with the stock. Bring to a boil and skim off any gray foam that rises.

2. Add the bay leaf and the ham bone, if using. Add the diced serrano ham and lard or butter.

3. Bubble up the stock again, reduce the heat, and cover. Leave to bubble gently for 1 hour or until the beans are perfectly soft (the time it takes depends on the age of the beans). Add boiling water as necessary to maintain the volume.

4. Mix the polenta with a little cold water and stir it into the soup. Bring back to a boil and bubble for 20 minutes more, or until the polenta has thickened the broth. Taste and season with salt and pepper.

5. Ladle into deep soup bowls and garnish each portion with crumbled blue cheese.

WELSH OATMEAL CAWL

The cawl is a soup of variable composition that is often served in more than one course. Ingredients are variable and seasonal, and can include any combination of vegetables, grains, and meat. The only rule is that everything is cooked in the pot without any preliminary frying. This version is from the Brecon Beacons in South Wales.

SERVES 4–6

1¹⁄₂ quarts ham or bacon stock
   (see page 15)
2 heaped tablespoons coarse ground
   oatmeal
1lb potatoes, peeled and diced
¹⁄₂lb rutabaga or parsnip, diced
¹⁄₂lb carrots, diced
2 large leeks, thinly sliced
Salt
¹⁄₂ stick (4 tablespoons) chilled butter
   (optional)
1 tablespoon each chopped fresh
   parsley and chives, to garnish

1. Put the stock in a saucepan and stir in the oatmeal. Bring to a boil, stirring until smooth. Add the prepared vegetables and bring back to a boil. Reduce the heat to a simmer. Cook gently for about 30 minutes, or until the vegetables are soft and the oatmeal has thickened the broth. Taste and add salt if necessary.

2. Serve in deep soup bowls (wooden bowls and spoons are traditional) and put a curl of butter into each bowl just before serving, if liked. Garnish with chopped parsley and chives.

MULLIGATAWNY WITH DHAL

A smooth lentil soup made with yellow or orange dhal—or any of the wide variety of dhals available to Indian cooks. The mulligatawny is an invention of Tamil cooks who added meat to a vegetarian lentil-and-rice combination, kichdee, to please their employers, the beef-eaters of the British Raj.

SERVES 4–6

½ cup yellow or orange lentils

⅓ cup long-grain rice

1½ quarts chicken stock (see page 16)

1 tablespoon curry powder or garam masala

½ stick (4 tablespoons) butter

2 onions, thinly sliced

2 garlic cloves, sliced

3–4 cloves

1 short cinnamon stick, broken into small pieces

Salt and ground black pepper

TO SERVE

1 cup plain yogurt stirred with chopped fresh mint

Poppadoms or crispy toasted or fried Bombay duck, if liked

1. Pick over and rinse the lentils and put them and the rice in a saucepan with the stock. Bring to a boil. Skim off the gray foam that rises, then stir in the curry powder or garam masala. Reduce the heat and leave to simmer gently for about 1 hour, or until the dhal is perfectly tender and soupy. Season with salt and a generous amount of freshly ground black pepper.

2. Meanwhile, melt the butter in a frying pan. As soon as it froths, add the onions, garlic, cloves, and cinnamon, then fry gently until soft and beginning to brown. Stir the contents of the pan into the soup and taste and adjust the seasoning.

3. Reheat and ladle into bowls. Separately, hand round a bowl of yogurt stirred with a handful of chopped mint leaves (chop the mint at the last minute).

4. Serve with poppadoms or crispy toasted or fried Bombay duck (a dried fish preparation available in Indian groceries), if liked.

POLISH BUCKWHEAT & MUSHROOM SOUP

A nutty buckwheat soup flavored with mushrooms and finished with sour cream—just the thing for a chilly fall evening. Buckwheat is the seed of a grass native to the steppes of Central Asia, which thrives in a cold climate. The scent is a little sweet, like newly mown hay, and the texture is pleasantly gritty.

SERVES 4–6

½lb whole buckwheat
½ stick (4 tablespoons) butter
2 quarts ham, vegetable, or chicken
   stock (see pages 15 and 16)
¾lb mushrooms (wild or cultivated),
   sliced
Salt and ground black pepper
TO GARNISH
1¼ cups soured cream
2 tablespoons chopped fresh dill
TO SERVE
Black bread
Unsalted butter
Fresh radishes or pickled cucumbers

1. Fry the buckwheat grains in half the butter in a medium saucepan for 2–3 minutes, or until they smell toasty. Add the stock and bring to a boil. Reduce the heat to a gentle simmer, cover tightly, and cook for 40–50 minutes, or until the grains are soft and "porridgy" (add boiling water if they begin to look dry).

2. Meanwhile, melt the remaining butter in a small frying pan. Add the mushrooms and season with salt and pepper. Toss them over the heat until the fungi yield up their water and begin to fry. Stir the contents of the frying pan into the soup when the buckwheat is soft.

3. Ladle into bowls and garnish each portion with a dollop of sour cream and a sprinkle of chopped dill. Serve with black bread, unsalted butter, and fresh radishes or pickled cucumbers.

INDEX